A MAP THROUGH THE MAZE

A Guide to S[...]
the Criminal Jus[...]

Ned Rollo with

Louis W. Adams, D.Min.

Katherine S. Greene
(Open, Inc. Information Series Editor)

IMPACT PUBLICATIONS
Manassas Park, VA

ISBN: 978-1-57023-353-1 (paperback); 978-1-57023-371-5 (eBook)

Library of Congress: 2015932907

Publisher: For information on Impact Publications, including current and forthcoming publications, authors, press kits, online bookstore, and submission requirements, visit the left navigation bar on the front page of the company's main website: www.impactpublications.com.

Quantity Discounts: We offer quantity discounts (20-60%) on bulk purchases. For details, visit www.impactpublications.com or contact the Special Sales Department: Tel. 703-361-7300 or query@impactpublications.com.

Publicity/Rights: For information on publicity, author interviews, and subsidiary rights, contact the Media Relations Department: Tel. 703-361-7300, Fax 703-335-9486, or email: query@impactpublications.com.

Sales/Distribution: All bookstore sales are handled through Impact's trade distributor: National Book Network, 15200 NBN Way, Blue Ridge Summit, PA 17214, Tel. 1-800-462-6420. All special sales and distribution inquiries should be directed to the publisher: Sales Department, IMPACT PUBLICATIONS, 9104 Manassas Drive, Suite N, Manassas Park, VA 20111-5211, Tel. 703-361-7300, Fax 703-335-9486, or email: query@impactpublications.com.

Contents

New Realities

The Correctional Experience

Dedication

Dedicated to HENRY LANGER
A friend, client, benefactor,
and exceptionally good man,
Who paid his dues, took control,
and put the past behind him.
Rest in peace.

Foreword

SINCE 1970, when as a young ex-convict he worked in a hostel for ex-prisoners in the Hyde Park district of Chicago where my family and I make our home, I have admired Ned Rollo and his dedication to helping those leaving prison make a useful life for themselves and for us.

In *A Map Through the Maze* he distills the knowledge and experience gained from his long and interesting journey of service. He knows whereof he writes, and he writes in a sprightly and compelling manner. He used his own bootstraps and a fine intelligence to pull himself up to a contributing life after five and a half years in prison; he now teaches others how to achieve five years of arrest-free behavior as the means of escape from the maze of convicthood.

Self-image is the key; but self-image is to be shaped not by wishing it were so but by behaving so that it **is** so. The path Rollo has cleared for others to follow is shaped both by practical realities and by a sound psychological understanding.

It is a pleasure to be associated with this book. It stands in a noble tradition of respect for human endeavor, for recognition that there is a spark in all men and women that can be fanned to help shape a good life.

Norval Morris, Ph.D.
Professor of Law and Criminology
University of Chicago - 1993
(Dr. Morris departed this world in 2004)

A Note From the Hills

Ned Rollo

Wild Hog
Ridge

A COOL, RAINY night. Typical for autumn deep in the Ozark Mountains. The hummingbirds headed south last week and soon the first freeze will silence the night creatures, sending this isolated world into a deep stillness until reborn again next spring. For ten winters I have chosen to live as a forest dweller, a hermit of sorts, in the cusp of a one-mile long crescent moon valley along the banks of a quiet, crystal clear river.

Decades of commitment were required to take control of my 200 acres of raw mountain land. As with many former prisoners, it was a dream of privacy and a way to "get clean" which sustained me though prison and beyond. Thus I came here to create a sanctuary, building a "man cave" safe from the rain and wind, in tune with nature and set apart from the prying eyes of the ever shrinking world. I share this with you for one reason: as proof that it is possible to radically alter your reality for the better; to transform a heart-sustaining ambition into reality. It **can** be done.

Now, with another winter fast approaching, I have finally finished this 2nd edition of *A Map Through the Maze* as a modest gift to all the folks of the world who greet dawn through the bars of a cage. And after a half century of closely watching people endure the soul-shattering experience of human captivity, I have but one suggestion appropriate for all: own yourself! Never surrender hope or allow the urge to dive into darkness consume you.

In a cell, on a street corner or a mountain top, we all hunger for a way to be useful, to feel fulfilled, to be worthy of trust, and be at peace. On behalf of myself and Katherine Greene, my partner and dearest friend, we sincerely hope this book may assist those called upon to endure the adversity of captivity and, ever further, achieve happiness as constructive elements in the complex world we all share. Be well!

Introduction

A MAP THROUGH THE MAZE is a self-change guide written to encourage and assist people locked in cages, as well as their loved ones who often suffer along with them in the free world. Before deciding to read this, you will want to know why it was created. Perhaps I can best explain this through a process of elimination...by defining who I, Ned Rollo, am not.

I am not the government or any branch thereof. I am not a puppet of any political or social agenda. Nor am I a naive do-gooder who wants to take you under my wing or "fix" you. I am not here to harvest souls, remold personalities, or jack with the minds and hearts of prisoners.

Last, I don't plan to bore you with theories or judgments as to how you "ought" to think and live. Instead, I speak directly to the mental and emotional frame of mind required to endure life in the dark heart of the punishment experience. My job is straightforward: To tell you the truth as I have grown to understand it...the good, the bad, and the ugly...and to point the way to a better path, in the event you wish to follow it.

The good news is that beauty, kindness, comfort, and peace of mind actually exist. Above all, they can be achieved! This reality represents a wellspring from which powerless people, flushed and forgotten by society, can draw hope of a better day. Underlying this book is the certainty that **life after prison really is worth living**. And whatever **price** you must pay during and following captivity, the **rewards** are well worth the investment required.

A Map Through the Maze offers a down-to-earth view of what it takes to cope with the mental and emotional quicksand of the American correctional circus. This is not about the superficial concerns anyone can observe on a fish bowl tour through a state or federal joint. Rather it offers a personal frame of reference for dealing with the deep-seated, toxic effects of waking up a thousand mornings in a concrete tomb.

What is covered here is not so much about the mechanics of doing time. Prisoners and their people already know a lot about that! More important is a practical world view that can help a person navigate through the madness of the maze. My goal is to help you define and apply the perspective needed to survive this unique life experience and, in so doing, prepare to prosper afterwards. To actually apply all this to a positive end!

Like the experience of squatting naked in the corner of a solitary cell, this book is **stark reality.** You will not like everything it offers, but don't waste the opportunity to benefit from it! *A Map Through the Maze* reaches far beyond mere survival. It is about building a rewarding life against all odds, both now and later. About making constructive use of negative events and lessons in order to grow into a better, wiser, more productive, and more fulfilled human being.

If you are expecting the views and opinions of outside observers or well-intended "squares," this book will surprise you. It is much more than a collection of war stories, complaints about injustice, or wishful projections of how things are supposed to be. Instead, we focus here on ways to achieve and maintain **freedom,** the most basic concern of every prisoner in the world. To do this we look at what freedom means, how to build it, and how to keep it. The contents are based on the direct experiences and insights of thousands of outlaws and social rejects: some who died in a cage and others who are living well in the free world.

Freedom is a complex issue. The liberty to think and do as we wish is one of the great ambitions of all humans. Yet we tend to appreciate it most when we have it least. And too often it is more an illusion than a fact. In reality, freedom is never total, and it is surely never free. But for the legions of men and women under lock and key this hour, greater freedom is the main goal of daily life. Not just physical liberty, but freedom of mind and spirit as well.

Once defined as a criminal and locked away from the world, you find yourself at the bottom of a 1,000-foot well. Looking up from that dark, frightening place, the universe is but a tiny dot of light. It takes great **courage and supreme commitment** to slowly climb to the surface and feel again the joy of a spring breeze or a child's smile.

First you must learn to master the heavy, insane changes that come with the American process of justice. From arrest, through court and captivity, to long after release, the journey often seems an endless maze of barriers and deadly traps. People labeled as criminals wage a constant battle to survive. Theirs is an uphill path of fear, fragile hope, and daily distress. To succeed takes unique insight, determination, and skill. But it **can** be done.

Along with the plight of prisoners, we have a special concern for families and loved ones who try so hard and give up so much. Those who struggle to stand by a prisoner are often totally alone and taken for granted. They are called upon to perform legal miracles, drive 12 hours to spend one hour with a hostile, depressed inmate, and, on top of everything else, not complain. So, for those who love a prisoner and are expected to jump tall buildings, send money, and write every day, this book is for you as well! Keep it close by to review when you feel lost. It will improve your well-being and peace of mind.

Family members and loved ones who study this book will increase their understanding of the changes an inmate goes through. It offers a glimpse inside the head of prisoners as they move from one stage and mood to another. This helps reduce some of the stress of wondering what's going on and why. At the same time, inmates who study it will better grasp the intense pressures faced by their loved ones as they wait and worry.

Thus, *A Map Through the Maze* is a very special guidebook. It offers training and support to solve a unique series of problems, cope with hardship, and maintain hope against all odds. It includes practical insight into the mental and social changes people go through and the outlook needed to cope with extreme adversity. But beyond mere endurance, this is a guide to obtaining true freedom through personal growth of mind and heart.

To help you exit this crazy trip stronger, wiser, and in greater control over your future, this material is broken into four parts. First, an inmate's look at the nature of freedom. Next, how to "beat the system" through personal growth. Third, a hard-core tour through the correctional experience. And, last, some very special advice on how families and loved ones can overcome grief, hold on, and get healthy.

1

The Nature of Freedom

*"Man, freedom is being able to saddle up
and ride off into the sunset!"*

Just Cut Me Loose!

ASK ANY PRISONER what he or she wants more than anything else and the answer is automatic: "OUT!" Nose first or toes first, **everyone wants to be free!**

Most people would say that freedom means being able to do what you want, when you want. Yet, if you stop and look at it, this is romantic nonsense. **Reality never permits us to be totally free.** What we do always has limits, both in the joint and in the free world. Laws of nature restrict what we can do physically, in addition to the social boundaries created by the people and society around us. Not everyone can be president, walk on the moon, make a million dollars, or gain the love of the person they desire.

Freedom will always be limited because we can't control the forces of nature, the rules of society, or the choices of other people. However, between the extremes of total liberty and total slavery, there is a vast area where we can govern our own fate. This is especially true of the ways we treat ourselves and others and of the values we choose to live by. While we always seek maximum freedom, the quality of our lives will be determined by how well we strike a **balance** between our desires and the limits of reality.

To someone in a cage, this may sound crazy: as long as the door is locked, there can be no freedom. But nothing could be further from the truth. Yes, they **do** have your body, that's a fact. But **not** your mind or spirit...those are **yours!** Regardless of the condition of your body, you have the ability to choose how you will live inside your own head. This process requires taking an honest look at who and what you are and learning to exercise maximum control over your thoughts, feelings, and actions.

Free But Not Free

What if a person had all the money, power, and possessions they could desire, and society would let them do as they pleased: would they then be truly free? No, it would still be an **illusion** because our freedom is limited from birth by the certainty that we will die. No one is free from aging, suffering, and death.

And even if we could be free of all these external chains, we can still be enslaved by ourselves. Our thoughts and feelings, desires and fears can entrap us just as surely as steel bars. Let's get one thing straight: we cannot be "free" if we insist on surrendering our well-being to anything or anyone outside ourselves, to any of the countless things we use to "make us feel better," "take the edge off," or "make the pain go away." After all is said and done, the only meaningful freedom is our ability to accept responsibility for what we think and do and the results of those thoughts and actions.

So our level of freedom depends not just on the condition of our body and the world we live in, but also on the state of our mind and what we carry within us: what we think and how we feel about ourselves and everything around us. If we don't learn to control how we think, feel, and react, then we are mere robots, directed by whatever ideas, emotions, and desires run through or around us.

For instance, no matter where you are, if you are eaten up with anger or greed, you are not free. Why? Because you are controlled by the force of that rage and lust within yourself. Your choices and actions are based on those powerful emotions – not on what is best for you or most truly fulfills your goals and intentions. You may really desire close, loving relationships, but if anger runs your life, you will wall yourself off from others and drive them away. As long as such negative emotions control you, you are not free to be the person you want to be.

As another example, if you build your life on falsehood, on what you imagine things to be rather than what they really are, you become a slave to illusion. You may be free to make choices, but your freedom is limited because you don't really understand yourself or the world around you. As long as your view of yourself and the world is distorted, you will be a captive of your own ignorance.

So "freedom" is only a word until we face the traps hiding within ourselves. Why dream of the day of release if in the process we collect centuries worth of hostility, fear, distrust, false goals, and self-hatred? In reality, we build our own personal prison and sentence ourselves to death by lethal aloneness. There has to be a better way! And there is!

True Freedom

"True freedom comes when you see through falsehood and respond to life and yourself as they really are."

Just as we can be slaves to the world or to ourselves, we also can achieve immense freedom! Although external liberty often depends on what the world around us will allow, our internal freedom is based on the health and power of our own minds and wills. In fact, the only thing we can truly control is ourselves! True freedom is possible as we come to honest terms with ourselves and dedicate our efforts to personal growth and positive action.

To be truly free, we must learn to "own" our thoughts and feelings, not be owned by them. We have to stand up and refuse to be trapped in hate, fear, lust, or knee-jerk reactions to outside events. We must accept the fact that "there ain't no free lunch," and not fool ourselves with distorted ideas. No matter what your immediate status in the system, now is the perfect time to look at yourself and the world clearly and honestly, so your thoughts and actions are based on fact, not illusion.

Since prisoners are social outcasts, you must remember that your true power and worth exist within yourself. Your quality is not based on what other people think or do. Instead, it depends on the nature of your inner self and the values you carry within, no matter if your body is in a lockdown cell in Leavenworth or on a sun-drenched beach in the South Pacific.

When someone commands your body, they have the least of you; but if they control your mind or break your spirit, they have ALL of you! For this reason, you must be ever vigilant. Always respect your mind and heart and be ready to protect them from confusion and illusion, whether created by you or by outside forces.

When you don't know what you stand for, someone else can come into your head and shove you around. But when you have a clear picture of what's real and what you believe in, people have a hard time pushing your buttons! Once you have your own internal rules clearly defined, you can learn to adapt to the rules of both prison and the streets without losing your identity, dignity, or self-worth.

Remember: you can't control what happens – in the maze or in the world – but you can control how you think about and react to it. This is the secret to freedom in an unfree world!

A clear mind with truth as its goal is one of the most important qualities we can develop in the quest for a rewarding life. Without it, all the physical freedom and fortune in the world mean nothing. While our bodies exist on limited levels, the scope of our minds and spirits is boundless. We are capable of an infinite variety of possible paths.

With the right direction and force of will, we can cast aside the chains of ignorance and suffering and learn to soar. *"Come on, even in a stinking cage?"* Yes, even in the darkest, foulest dungeon on this planet!

Making Yourself Free

While mankind has learned to make atomic bombs and send rovers to Mars, the ability to direct our thoughts and values is the greatest power we have. Although outside forces may hold, chain, or even torture us, they cannot control our minds unless we surrender them! In the end, this most powerful form of freedom is beyond the grasp of anyone outside us. But the only way we can access it is through dedication and hard work. It cannot be bought or stolen. No one else can give it to us, and likewise no one can take it away, unless we refuse to meet our responsibility to ourselves and others.

You don't have to be a genius to be mentally free. But you must learn to tell the difference between fact and falsehood, between what is real and what is not, and then be willing to follow the truth. In a world that is 99% jive, finding the 1% that is real is the basis for true freedom. Then you need the honesty, courage, and willpower to apply your insight in positive, productive ways. **Your hard-won wisdom will be meaningless until you put it to positive use.**

To do this, in prison or on the streets, we must constantly practice self-discovery and self-mastery. To free our minds, we have to seek out truth and wisdom. This requires that we openly test what we believe, discard what we find to be false, and then adopt what is more factual and useful. The greatest thief of our freedom is our own false thinking and narrow vision.

For example, many of us were raised with strong biases against people of different races or beliefs. This keeps us apart from others, creating unnecessary fear, suspicion, and even hate. Yet as adults we often meet someone of a different color or religion who is honest, decent, and good. We may find, to our shock, that we actually like and respect this person, although we were raised to distrust him or her.

How do we come to terms with this conflict of our past ideas and the present reality? We must examine ourselves, question the things we were raised blindly to believe, then seek to discover how things really are and how they should be. Our capacity to sort out true from false and right from wrong is unique to the human mind. And this ability offers a kind of freedom far more powerful than anything on a physical plane.

Stop and look within. As you move through the stages of the criminal justice system, you will come across parts of yourself that are enslaved by ideas contrary to fact. You will not want to change and may strongly resist coming to terms with truth and justice; this is just part of human nature. But it is essential that you have the courage, strength, and flexibility required to change...to get up and grow.

A Choice to Grow

"The choice is simple: grow or die."

Being a "guest of the government" can drive you crazy, but it can also "drive you sane" in unique ways. There is nothing like a jailhouse to help you examine your views and values. While free-world folks are busy with concerns such as the tread on their tires and braces on a kid's teeth, prisoners and their loved ones often deal with sheer get-down survival and cold-blooded reality.

Just as life in prison calls time-out on trivial everyday issues, it also brings you face to face with the here and now. In so doing, it offers a chance to stop and think. To reflect on the nature of life and your place in it. It demands that you get real and get right!

Hard times in general force you to look into the deeper parts of yourself. But it is an even greater challenge when your vision is distorted by the madness of the maze. It takes super-human dedication and effort to grow tall enough mentally to see over the mountains of emotional garbage, brick walls, and rows of razor wire which confine you. Whenever you find something is keeping you lost in darkness and confusion, dedicate yourself to finding a better path, no matter how much effort it requires. What a grand opportunity to stand up on your toes and look over what is blocking your view!

Part of the wonderful power of our minds and hearts is the ability to change what we think, what we value, and how we react. When we find something that just isn't true or doesn't work, we have what it takes to alter our beliefs and responses. And as we grow mentally and spiritually, we develop the wisdom to see and respond to things **as they truly are**. This is what's required to find a way out of the current trap and never come back.

Growth in a cage requires limitless courage and sweat, but great progress is possible! Throughout history, times of imprisonment and hardship have driven people to discover and focus their inner spirit. I am referring to something much deeper, more honest and real than simply running a game on some gullible church folks.

Spiritual awareness is the extension of our minds beyond time and space into the highest levels of being we humans are capable of. One truly positive aspect of fighting through the criminal justice jungle is making use of this painful, nasty experience to expand our grasp of our higher nature.

As you know, captivity is too long, hard, and dangerous for anyone to survive and exit without immense courage, honesty, and discipline. So, unless you are content to live and die as human roadkill, you have no choice but to pay the price and unlock the freedom of your mind and spirit!

In the next section, we will look at what it takes to grow beyond your current plight and ultimately put it behind you. Above all else, you must remember that **it can be done and you can do it!**

2

Beating the System

"Listen, bro, beating these fools is the name of this game!"

EVERY CONVICT SEARCHES for ways to defeat the "system" – or, too often, anything or anybody they can get their hooks into. But just how does a person **really** get past the system? I've asked myself this question for half a century. Do you become a jailhouse lawyer or a militant reformer, dig a hole under the east wall, or do scams over the pay phones? Or are there better ways? Just what does one have to do to "beat the system"?

First of all, if you go to serious war with the Man, what happens? In comes the goon squad in body armor to strum on your head. If it's a riot, up drives the state police and 66 loads of SWAT. If that doesn't do the trick, up pops the national guard, anxious to drop the hammer. The body count is always the same. The Man: a few, mostly bystanders. Convicts: many, most also just bystanders. Therefore, direct physical assault achieves nothing but a bloodbath. Plus it gives the administration an excuse to tighten the screws yet another turn!

Listen, I am NOT saying you should just roll over and play dead. But be careful not to draw your sword and step off into quicksand. Maintaining your dignity is one thing, but setting yourself up for a fresh dime or a load of #00 buckshot is counter-productive. If you really think that making your problems worse is a way to make them better, I suggest you reconsider.

In the end, if you really want to "beat" anyone or anything, two things are needed: **you've got to outlive them and outgrow them!** This means using every drop of energy and every opportunity to improve yourself **on every possible level**. Until you move beyond the thinking and acting which lead to captivity (or addiction or whatever), you are doomed to remain a resident of some high-security tomb with well polished floors.

My personal concern, and equal concern for you, is how to best "go forward"? How do we, given our past attitudes and actions and the shadow of a criminal history, actually "get up and **get a life**"!?! First, how do we take control of what we think and do? And what is required to achieve a constructive, rewarding place for ourselves? These are the fundamental questions!

Growth is the Key

"Change is certain; growth is optional."

Change is Certain

Going to prison is like being sent to a hostile alien planet, where you face a long series of extreme hardships and strange, unnatural ways of thinking and acting. It's a three-shift graveyard full of distant memories and false dreams. A prisoner looks around and thinks, *"There ain't nothing happening here but fools talking trash!"* And, in fact, all you actually see and hear are people constantly shuffling to cope with day-to-day survival and bone-breaking boredom.

But that's only on the surface of things. While every day brings the same endless routine, what's going on **inside** of people never stands still. Like any war zone, a prison is a place which **demands** change! The question is, what types of changes are going to occur inside of **you**? Will they be positive or negative? Useful or harmful? Will you come out of it better able to cope and be content, or end up a broken-down basket case?

Growth is Optional

"Improvise, adapt, overcome."
– Unofficial motto of the U.S. Marine Corps

Simply existing and watching yourself get old doesn't take any special talent. It happens all by itself. The real challenge is having the will and skill to make use of change to advance yourself and make your life more rewarding. This advancement or positive change is what we are going to call "growth." It is the most powerful tool a convict has, both during and after prison.

Lying around in prison feeling like a zombie, you may believe personal development is impossible, that the best you can hope to do is make it from hour to hour. This is a normal result of grief and depression, but in reality nothing could be further from the truth. Fact: if we are not **actively** working to control and use the constant changes we experience, then we have surrendered our lives and become mere zoo animals. Growth is so much more than mere existence! Just existing – letting your fingernails grow while the rest of you stays in a coma – is like being dead but too lazy to fall over.

Listen to me: the way to **really** beat the Man is to **grow** – to expand your mind, body, and spirit. This means learning to control and direct yourself in order to rise above the madness and sadness of the moment. For a "slave of the state," **personal growth is the one and only path to success!**

There is no magical switch you can flip and suddenly you're on top of the growth game. Rather, **growth is a process of becoming**. Becoming more! This means active, determined pursuit of knowledge, understanding, and better ways of doing things. To truly grow, you must seek out new ways to make yourself ever more useful, content, and glad to be alive. In this way you celebrate life NOW, even from inside a steel cage. Why bother? Because the **rewards are progress and pride**.

You Must Decide

"I owe it to myself to develop my potential to the greatest degree possible."

Expand or shrink: the choice is yours. And it has to be faced **daily**. No other single decision has as great an impact on the outcome of life. In fact, it is this very choice that allows you to seek true freedom and power, in prison and in the world.

As a prisoner, you have little control over what you do and how you do it. Your options are very limited. But you do have total control over your decision to pursue personal development rather than sit around and decay. This advancement can be academic, vocational, artistic, spiritual, cultural, emotional, or in many other areas. Much can be achieved by simply taking an honest look into yourself. What happened? Why am I here? Now what!? The point is that you deliberately decide to apply your mind and energy to positive, creative issues.

Everyone faces this choice. But why do some fight to grow, even under the worst of conditions, while others simply give up? This is one of the great riddles of life. But the answer is the key it takes to unlock your shackles. Therefore it is worth whatever price must be paid to discover your own answer.

The Source of Power

"The power of a mind totally committed exceeds any other force on earth."

Overcoming the past demands determination and consistent application – an inner passion to focus on personal growth. Without this focus, the negative forces in and around us will decide who and what we are. And the world will look on and say, *"Poor Joe. He never had a chance."* No – poor Joe never stood up and made a chance for himself.

The quest for freedom demands a **total commitment** to doing our best with the cards we have been dealt. There must be an inner motivation to grow, to become the best that we can be. No one knows why this drive is stronger in some people than in others, but it is the central reason that we see some people achieve success while others fall short.

People have lots of excuses for not getting up and taking control of their lives. Many folks have a poor education, bad upbringing, lack of family support, physical or mental disabilities. But most problems can be resolved, partly if not entirely.

There are blind lawyers, one-legged skiers, paraplegic horseback riders, mentally impaired students, and successful ex-cons. Overcoming obstacles can be done! But it requires patience, determination, and hard work. There is no free lunch!

In reality, there is **no** excuse for refusing to develop our abilities and interests. In the long run, it isn't any easier to sit around waiting to die than it is to get up and make something happen. Yes, self-growth takes discipline, courage, and consistent effort. But not doing so means we have to face the same problems over and over again. Our problems never go away until we learn to solve them. In general, they just keep on getting worse. If you're going to be facing problems anyway, you might as well put your energy into solving them, rather than wasting time trying to escape.

Stop and consider: you owe it to yourself to make your life positive and rewarding. No doubt it's hard to improve your education, but it's even harder to make a living without doing so. It's not easy keeping fit and healthy, but it's sure better than being sick and weak. And if you put your energy into exploring life rather than trying to hide from it, you are rewarded by an expanding sense of achievement. This is a prize you can look forward to when you get tired and start wondering why you're pushing yourself so hard.

No Escape From Ourselves!

"Insanity is doing the same thing over and over again, but expecting different results." – Albert Einstein

To cultivate a rewarding future, we have to start where we are. Although we may not be satisfied with our current situation, the person we are this moment is the raw material for our transformation. If our past behavior has been unrewarding or hurtful for us and the people around us, then it's time to find a better way to interact with reality!

One area in our lives where we can always improve is problem-solving. The demands of life, both in prison and on the streets, are often complex and overwhelming. Being in a state of crisis doesn't allow us a lot of time and patience; every situation seems to demand an instant response. When this pressure gets great enough, we often blow up and do the first thing that occurs to us in order to get immediate relief.

This knee-jerk reaction helps relieve the stress, and it may even fix or postpone the problem for a while. But many situations, feelings, and problems have no instant solution. And when we react out of desperation, we often create new problems to face in the future. The original problem is not solved, only delayed; it will come back to haunt us even worse than before. And we forfeit the growth, pride, and peace of mind that come when we solve a problem and move on.

Reacting to the here-and-now without regard for the long-term effects of our actions is not effective problem-solving – **it just doesn't work**. Too often it is a trap, causing us to repeat the same behavior over and over again. Humans have a bad habit of thinking that if something doesn't work the first time, then we should do more of it. It is amazing the effort we will make to continue old ways of thinking and acting which hurt us, rather than face the fear and discomfort of trying something new. And the deeper and older the issues, the more we hold on to how things have always been.

To make things even worse, we feel like a failure when we don't solve the problem. The feeling of being a loser may be the worst result of all. It follows us like a black cloud, constantly affecting how we see ourselves. In this deadly state of mind, we can lose hope of making any real progress. If this occurs, we become our own jailers, trapped in a cycle of self-destructive behavior.

We all fall into this trap from time to time. Such counter-productive action is especially obvious when we are addicted to some substance, thought process, emotional rush, or controlling behavior. We use addictive behavior to relieve our stress, but it won't make our problems go away. While it may take the edge off, it doesn't solve anything! Our demons eventually reappear, plus we have to cope with new problems (physical, financial, legal, and in our relationships) created by the addiction itself.

If this is the story of your life, it's time for a change. Constructive change is always demanding – and it can be very frightening. But, in the end, **there's no escape**. You can keep on struggling with the same old issues, which keep getting worse, or you can put all that wasted energy into efforts to control and improve your fate. You owe it to yourself, and to the people who care about you, to choose the path toward growth and freedom.

Barriers to Growth

"The day you quit beating your head against the wall,
you begin to feel better immediately!"

Making a commitment to improve your life allows you to focus and work toward a better future. But it definitely won't be easy, because humans have a natural resistance to new ways of doing things. No matter how hurtful they are, our old ways are familiar; they seem to offer comfort and security. So doing away with them can be deeply disturbing.

In order to carry out your commitment to yourself, you will have to overcome many of the barriers listed below.

1. **Fear** is a powerful enemy of positive change. It can come in many forms, such as fear of failure, fear of rejection, fear of the unknown, even fear of change itself. In a way, when we think about changing a basic belief or pattern of behavior, it seems as if we will have to give up our true selves. We may fear change almost the way we would fear dying. Or we may not believe that we can be the same person if we change the way we think and act.

    Solution: One way to confront fear is to ask yourself what is the worst that could happen if your fear comes true. Many times, this is no worse than what you have now. Then decide what is the best possible outcome if you face your fear. Once you confront the worst that can happen, concentrate on the positive outcomes you can achieve by overcoming your fears. Realize that the person you are working to become is truly you; you are just freeing up more of your true self. Keep these thoughts in mind so that you can control your fear rather than it controlling you.

2. **Denial** is a defense mechanism we use to block out ideas we aren't prepared to deal with. It is a mental trick that keeps us from facing reality and making the changes we need to become better people. If we don't admit to ourselves that we have a problem or limitation, we tend to just glide along until something forces us to deal with it. Denial is a real "devil," because it keeps us content with and trapped in our own ignorance!

   Solution: Be painfully honest with yourself. And if someone suggests you have a problem, take heed; don't just blow it off or make excuses. Other people can sometimes see what is going on in your life more clearly than you can. Above all, don't be discouraged by admitting you have problems or issues that need work; this is the first step to solving them. In the end, it takes ten times more energy to ignore the true nature of things than it does to face reality and take positive action.

3. **Impatience** is an age-old barrier to growth. By wanting too much too soon, we set ourselves up to fail. This is a major trap in and out of prison and the source of much anxiety, both short- and long-term, for ex-convicts and their loved ones.

   Solution: Break each goal down into small achievable tasks. Then you will have a sense of achievement as you complete each step. It is much like building a house – one small project, then another, and another. Remind yourself that it takes time to make positive changes. The process can't be rushed along based on your wishes. Time will never bend itself to your needs, so you have to plan ahead and use it to your advantage. When you decide to take many small steps, change becomes your friend and ally.

4. **Unrealistic Goals** set us up to fail by focusing our energy on things that we probably can't achieve or things that will harm us, rather than help. Trying to do the impossible only keeps us from achieving what is possible. It wastes the energy we need for growth.

   Solution: Always remember that wanting what you cannot or should not have is the Number One enemy of all prisoners and loved ones. Test your goals with intense honesty and seek advice from people who have wisdom, maturity, and direct experience. Above all: think long and hard before you make a decision or base your hopes on anyone or anything.

5. **Addictions** or dependencies drain us of the power and mental focus we need to change and grow. We must free ourselves from any such anchors in order to best face the future.

   Solution: First, overcome your denial and admit the effect your addiction is having on you. Then seek help to gain control over the forces which command you.

Such problems seldom (if ever) go away by themselves. They demand attention, work, support, and a great deal of courage and resolve. You **can** do it – and you'll be real glad you did!

6. **Fatal Attachments** to other people create a special form of addiction that keeps us distracted and drained of energy and focus. Doing time distorts how we see and value others. A relationship spinning out of control can be far worse than any drug habit. Unless balanced with truth and reality, it can lead to untold misery and despair.

   Solution: Look honestly at how you relate to people. If your relationships aren't positive, resolve to improve them. If you can't, then let them go. Learn what it takes to build a healthy, positive relationship (see Personal Ties in the section on Taking Action). Focus on and practice rewarding ways to deal with others so that you build true friendships. Remember, good friends support positive growth. They don't double-dare you to sabotage yourself.

7. **Anger, Guilt, Isolation, and Worry** are negative feelings which soak up our energy and focus it in a negative direction. Each is a form of baggage we've collected to defend ourselves from dealing with our hurts and fears. Although they seem unpleasant, these feelings can become very real addictions that we use to avoid facing reality. Then we end up wasting our power on useless battles rather than working to grow and prosper.

   Solution: Make the conscious decision to "let go" of past resentments and focus on future growth. This means working to replace anger with peace of mind, guilt with forgiveness, and isolation with a sense of oneness with all beings. Be optimistic; you can and will gradually redefine who and what you are!

8. **Hopelessness** is the greatest enemy to growth. Without hope, we tend to just give up and shut down. I saved this until last because it often occurs as a result of the collective problems stated above. We can afford to lose many things and still be able to function, but the loss of hope is the ultimate trap. As such it must be avoided at all cost!

   Solution: Reach down into your center, into the core of your spirit, to find your connection with the power and wonder of the universe. Call upon your primitive instincts for the strength of will to survive and prosper. Never surrender your faith in beauty and your commitment to making the very best of your life. Never give up!

You deserve the best life you can make for yourself. As you struggle to cope with the burdens of captivity, expect to experience some, if not all, of these barriers as you focus on personal development. At times the barriers to change will seem overwhelming, but you must stick with it. One reward will be the intense satisfaction of knowing how hard you had to work for your progress.

Inside the Razor Wire

"Humpty Dumpty sat on the wall,
Humpty Dumpy took a GREAT fall.
All the King's horses and all the King's men
couldn't put Humpty together again."
– But Humpty could...**and he did!**

In order to solve problems and make positive changes, we first need to know how. In many ways this is connected to how we see the world and our place in it. So let's consider the basic attitudes required to create a new window through which we view the universe.

Accept Yourself

No one is born with an instruction manual on being human. Who you are today is the result of your past: what you have observed and what you have been taught, as well as the choices you've made. Many of your attitudes and values were formed when you were very young, so you may have no real idea **why** you think and behave the way you do.

Sometimes your actions are positive, constructive, and rewarding; other times they are just the opposite. If you use your time in prison to examine your life honestly, you may find that some of your behavior has caused great harm for others as well as yourself. This can be very painful, but you can't change what happened in the past. Getting lost in a guilt trip or fantasies about what could have been is a huge waste of time. It just ties up all the energy you could put into **change**, making the future better.

In order to move forward, you first need to acknowledge who and what you are **now**. Until you come to grips with your real self – warts, wounds, and all – you can't begin to heal. Thus the essential first step is self-honesty.

Next, rather than dwelling on guilt or shame, view your past mistakes as something you had to live through to become a wiser person. At the same time, commit yourself to learning from them in order to do better next time. Screwing up is a natural part of life, but there's no reason to keep repeating the same errors – that's totally unacceptable.

Accept Responsibility

Just as it is wasteful to wallow in guilt or shame, it is equally useless to make excuses or blame our actions on someone or something else. There may be many reasons for what you have done, but in the final count, you are where you are because of the choices you made. And believe it or not, this is good. After all, if everything you do is somebody else's fault, then you will never be free and in control of your life.

Tattoo this across your brain: if you don't want someone else running your show, **you have to do it for yourself**. When you waste energy trying to avoid responsibility for yourself, you become weaker and more vulnerable to outside control by the State and by other people and things. Many folks surrender and just go with the flow, simply existing as a robot for the forces around them. Running your own show is serious business; you must take control of yourself if you want to develop and protect your freedom and dignity.

Since **you** are responsible for what you do, it's an ideal time to expand the will, skill, and insight needed to manage your own life. This requires you to learn to understand and control your values, feelings, and responses. As you do so, a little at a time, you will find more satisfaction in daily living and a greater sense of self-worth.

Understand Cause and Effect

The rule of reality which governs everything is the law of cause and effect. We have all heard the expressions *"you reap what you sow"* and *"what goes around comes around."* Nothing could be more true! In fact, the quality of our lives ultimately depends on how well we apply the law of cause and effect.

This is not some game we can play just when we feel like it. It is an inescapable fact of nature. *"Live by the sword, die by the sword"* is one direct example.

We tend to think we can beat the game, dodge the results. But cause and effect is always up and running, even when we don't see the effects directly or immediately. For example, people who are exposed to the AIDS virus (cause) may seem healthy for years before they develop cancers and other serious illnesses (effect).

There are no exceptions. The law of cause and effect is in force with each and every thought and action. The good news is that, once we learn which actions lead to positive results, we have the power to improve our fate and grow beyond the negative past. When we fully accept that **everything** we do will come back to us in some form, suddenly it makes sense to think good thoughts and do good deeds.

Once we recognize the hard-core reality of cause and effect, we hold a major key to unlocking a positive, rewarding future. It is a powerful, life-changing moment when we finally accept that our thoughts and actions ultimately control our fate. This is a two-edged sword: it makes us responsible for our failures as well as our successes, and it also offers the greatest hope for personal growth and fulfillment. If the future is based on what we do **now**, even if it is slow to show up, **we have the power to change things!** This is the basis for real freedom!

Seek the Right Path

So far we have been discussing **how** to accept responsibility for ourselves and change our lives for the better. But **what** are we going to become? What is the goal of our progress and growth?

This is where we must address our **values**, what we believe to be right, true, and important. Developing our values and beliefs is a deeply personal activity. And while others may tell us what values we ought to choose, and even punish us for making a different choice, the final decision is always up to each individual.

In India, 4,000 years ago, seekers of the right path had this to say about values:

> *"We are what our deep, driving desire is. As our deep, driving desire is,*
> *so is our will. As our will is, so is our deed. As our deed is, so is our*
> *destiny." (Brihadaranyaka IV.4-5)*

In other words, our values determine who we are and who we will become. But since everyone views life differently, how do we figure out what is really "right, true, and important"? As we examine past values and behavior and make choices on which direction our growth will take, we need to be aware that some ways of thinking and acting work better than others. By looking at human history we can see that some ways usually have "good" (constructive, helpful) results, while others almost always have "bad" (destructive, harmful) results.

Of all the advice for establishing good values, perhaps none is more practical or down-to-earth than the Golden Rule: *"Treat others as you want to be treated."* Living by the Golden Rule doesn't guarantee that you will be treated well by others, of course. But it **always** influences the kind of person you are and how you think of yourself. In addition, it adds to the good will available in the world and makes it possible for more positive things to happen for everyone.

Many people would say that love of God, country, and family are the most important principles to live by. Many would say that we should be generous, help others, and respect the needs of our neighbors. That it is more important to be honest, fair, and helpful to others than it is to simply take what we want out of life. These values are considered good because they usually have helpful, constructive results.

However, if we look at what people do, we often see different values in action. We see people for whom money and material possessions, or power and control over others, are the most important ideals. Some people find ways to get around the rules or bend them without breaking the law. Others don't care if they hurt people or break the law to get what they want. There are always such people – like vultures, always circling.

These values are more likely to be considered bad because their results are generally less helpful, even destructive. However, it seems as if these values would get us what we want faster and easier than being "good." So if we choose good values, what's in it for us?

First: a path out of the criminal justice maze. You stand a much better chance of getting out and staying out of prison through helpful actions than through harmful behavior. Also, you can expect much more peace of mind if you're not always looking over your shoulder for the law to grab you or figuring an angle to put something over on an unsuspecting person. You will find a greater degree of social acceptance for positive behavior than for negative actions. And you will end up with greater self-respect; positive thoughts and actions give us good feelings about ourselves, and this is what makes everything else worthwhile.

Understand, I'm not suggesting you put on a halo and run about doing good for everyone else at the expense of yourself. Instead, make constructive choices that bring about the most positive results for you and for those around you. **Look for ways to create an all-win situation.** Choose actions that allow you to fulfill your potential and produce something useful for yourself and others. Practice behavior that helps you build trust and form rewarding relationships with other people. Pursue thoughts and actions that make you feel worthwhile and at peace with yourself. In the end, That is what truly matters!

Eventually, you may find that your greatest personal satisfaction comes from knowing you have met your obligations – to other people as well as yourself – and that you have left the world a better place. This kind of gift to mankind will last far beyond your own life, while your possessions will just be items in a Saturday morning garage sale when you're gone.

Making the System Work for You

If you want to grow beyond the system, get started right now. There's no point in waiting till later. The day you hit the streets is way too late, so why not begin this very moment?

Look at it this way: prison isn't an experience to be wasted. Every moment is so twisted and destructive that it must be put to practical use in order to salvage some value from it. Rather than sitting around playing dominos or watching TV, why not focus on personal development? Improve your mind. Expand your ability to meet your needs, help others, and feel better about yourself. Can you think of any more meaningful way to beat the system?

Learning Through Hardship

As we've said, taking a fall helps a person stop and look at the direction and meaning of life. While citizens are concerned with Monday night football, you have a chance to examine the deepest parts of your mind and heart. What you find, you may not like. If that's the case, you have the time and opportunity to pull yourself together and **change it!**

Jails and prisons are places of intense pressure and, like all war zones, produce intense change. For better or worse, no one gets to stand still. What kind of shape are you going to be in when they finally kick you out? It may well depend on what direction you're taking this very moment.

Surviving and growing beyond the prison experience is not an easy task. In fact, it's more like a mental and physical obstacle course. It's dangerous and painful to go through, but it helps us develop greater strength and new skills. It takes time and effort to make it over the hurdles, but we sure have a clear knowledge of our abilities by the end of the course. So let's look at the state of mind and spirit needed to survive and grow from it all.

Reshape Your Thinking

As a prisoner, you may often feel like you're trapped in a revolving nightmare. But be aware that there are mental tools and ways of looking at things that can be your salvation. First, always remember that this situation had a beginning and will have an end. Even if it's in a pine box, you will get out. For most people, being labeled a criminal is only one chapter in life. It's really up to you if you want to take the brand of "outcast" to your grave. Surely it's not necessary! Even while you are locked up, you can develop different ways of thinking and acting that are those of a well-intentioned citizen worthy of respect. The secret is to learn new ways of thinking and to develop control over your thoughts and actions. This is an achievement of untold worth! Please consider the following facts:

1. You are human, not some wild animal driven by blind instinct. **Stop and think before you act!** Being controlled by the State is demanding, but learning to control yourself is a thousand times harder. There is no greater challenge anyone can face than coming to grips with their own thoughts, emotions, and behaviors. Learn to **watch** the way your mind works, **study** the effects, **control** your emotions, and you will learn to better **direct** your actions. In the process, you will gain an increasing ability to make positive changes in your life.

2. In most cases you are not limited to one fixed way of doing things: **You have choices.** Telling yourself that you cannot cope or have no way out leads to mental illness and spiritual decay. Be creative; make a list of **all** the possible ways to solve your problem. Reach out for positive ideas and new ways to cope. As you learn to look and listen, you'll discover that new options come from the most unexpected people and at the most unexpected times. Stay alert, be open to new ideas and ready to adapt.

3. As you review your options, consider the **possible outcomes** for each. Which one has the best chance of granting positive, winning results? I don't mean an instant, short-term fix but a real solution. Beware: anything that makes your problems worse is not a useful solution!

4. When it comes to solving problems, you must have plenty of **patience and faith.** Once you act on your decision, give it enough time to work. Expecting instant relief is a trap, because solutions occur in steps. It takes a lot of time and thought to make a decision and put it into action, so give it a serious chance to work.

5. Usually you have to deal with things in stages, like the seasons of the year. When working on a complex issue, you can **divide it into manageable parts** and better control the results. This is equally true for getting a job, overcoming an addiction, or making a good marriage. Spending time and energy to work through a problem helps you be and feel better prepared. No matter how big the task or ambitious your plans, it always comes down to one step at a time!

6. **Observe the results** of what you think and do. Use these outcomes to test your beliefs and modify your future actions. The only real failure is refusing to learn from your experiences. If you find that you keep making the same mistakes over and over, admit that you could use some help and begin looking for the best source. It's okay to seek help, because staying stuck in a rut of failure and frustration is unnecessary and a waste of time.

7. **Give yourself credit** for the progress you make. Celebrate your victories; take pride and satisfaction in every bit of achievement! And if you don't score a total success or things don't move as quickly as you'd like, just keep on cooking! Above all, never give up!

Use What's There!

*"Pounce on ANY source of positive energy
like a duck on a June bug!"*

To improve your chances of success, use your time to develop an attitude and a plan which will increase your sense of personal control and satisfaction. Any chance you have to grow by expanding your mind or skills, any counseling or support you can get, any steps you can take to improve yourself – **do it!** Prisons are not known for their abundance of culture and opportunity, but you can usually find access to educational courses or vocational training, libraries, self-help groups, or visits from outside volunteers. Whatever may be there, get up and use it!

If you don't know how to read very well, practice. Absorb everything you can get your hands on that improves your abilities and self-respect. Don't just kick back and get lost in romance novels, westerns, detective stories, or spy thrillers. While great for entertainment, they don't push you to grow. Read and study things that put your time and mind to work. You're looking for new, fresh ideas that make you think, not just movie or sports magazines that put you to sleep.

Once you make an unbending commitment to self-improvement and ultimate success, you can't afford to waste valuable time and energy on the garbage going on around you. This sense of purpose, linked with discipline, is priceless as you wade through the distractions and folly of life in prison or in the free world. Believe it or not, learning this one skill can make the disaster of imprisonment a valuable experience.

Ya Snapped Yet?

*"The freedom we seek begins with the decision to accept
responsibility for the gift of life we have been granted."*

A lot of what happens during and after prison depends on a person's attitude. Having a "bad attitude" usually means being negative, selfish, hostile, or just an overall pain in the butt. Such people are **no fun** to be around and usually self-centered to the bone. So folks who follow this approach set themselves up to be rejected.

But even worse, people with a bad attitude deceive and weaken themselves by blaming everything and everyone else for their problems. Because prison is a small world, everyone watches each other closely. They notice how people cope with what comes down. And they learn to identify those who deal with reality and those who don't. Some inmates deal with things head on, find solutions, and move on. Others snivel and moan, make up off-the-wall excuses to put their weight on somebody else, and try to wiggle out of any situation.

So what if your babysitter dropped you on your head when you were two? That didn't have anything to do with your knocking off a liquor store when you were 22! And it wasn't your girlfriend's fault because she wanted some Crown Royal and you didn't have the money. You know how it is; this ducking and dodging could go on forever. Let's get real: you did it because **you chose to!** It may have been a dumb decision, but, by God, your granny didn't do it, **you did!!**

So don't get caught in the trap of claiming that whatever comes down is someone else's fault! This is usually followed by a lot of self-pity, anger, hostility, and endless war talk as you sell yourself an ever-expanding lie. Such an approach is harmful because it keeps you from taking command of your fate and future. Therefore, it is a very powerful form of self-deception, in and out of the joint. To be truly free, you must be willing and able to be honest with yourself.

On the other hand, a "good attitude" is one that looks reality dead in the eye and comes up with positive, constructive steps that lead to progress, achievement, and satisfaction. A good attitude is one that works hard to exercise self-control and accepts the results, good and bad, as your personal property.

Think on this: if you don't accept responsibility for your actions and the results **here and now**, how are you going to control your future? After all, if someone or something else is always ruling your fate, that makes you just a life-long victim of circumstances, politics, luck, the full moon, etc. What do you have to gain from being a self-defined puppet?

Cut It All Loose!

---

*"Never give up responsibility for yourself
to ANYTHING beyond your control!"*

We tend to believe that whatever we need to be free and happy exists **outside of us** waiting to be captured or achieved. We think that if we can only get enough of something or someone, we will be happy. This idea that something outside ourselves can bring us true satisfaction has a major drawback: **it doesn't work!** People, places, and things outside of us can give us pleasure, but they are not the true source of happiness. That is something we must work out for ourselves.

It's easy to get hooked on other people or things – especially for prisoners looking for an escape from themselves and the pain and boredom of being locked up. We all know others who have gotten strung out on a variety of drugs, alcohol, risky activities (sticking a gun in somebody's face can be a real rush), or even food. There's nothing like a few Milky Ways to get pumped up for the yard.

Sometimes we want our sweets in human form, so we crave a person. We look up and **wham**, it's love (or lust) at first sight. We kiss, bells ring, and trees burst into bloom in mid-winter. Life is suddenly great. Then, without warning, he/she does an overnight marriage trip to Reno with our best friend, leaving us wanting to take a long walk off a short pier. **No good!**

What delights us one day often becomes a curse the next. We see this all the time in romantic relationships that self-destruct when one party fails to provide what the other party desires. Jailhouse romances are especially fragile because they take place long distance, based more on wishful thinking than reality.

Any effort to escape problems or base our happiness on something outside ourselves is just walking on quicksand. No such escape will last forever. After the high comes the letdown, and reality descends on us with a sickening thud. Plus, in the case of addiction, we have the added problem of craving more of the person, place, or thing even though it just makes thing worse!

In reality, whenever we give up responsibility for our own life to anything beyond our control, we surrender our freedom and cast ourselves into self-imposed slavery. This doesn't mean that we should avoid loving other people or caring about what happens around us. But we must remember that **all persons and things are subject to ongoing change**.

Although we can work to improve the odds in our favor, we can't control everything. "Control" is too often just an illusion. So we can never have any guarantee that we will get what we want or that things will stay the same. In order to be really free, we must know that we can live and even prosper without the things we desire. In short, we can **adapt**!

If you can achieve your desires, that's great. But be prepared to carry on and make the most of your life without them. Have faith in yourself that you can create something worthwhile out of any situation that comes to you. After all, if you can achieve positive results in a prison cell, you can do it anywhere. So quit hanging on to external sources of happiness. **What you need is already within you!** Your next step is to find an effective process of discovery and development. Time to get up and **do it!**

Taking Action

Planning for Battle

"He who's best prepared wins the war!"

FACT: surviving and exiting jail or prison is tough – and that's only half the battle. If you don't stay out, you lose! If the world eats you because you don't know how to cope, you lose! If you don't make life better than before, you lose!! Therefore, the better your preparation, the better your odds for being a winner.

Finding your way through the maze takes hard work and great resolve. Every new phase of the journey requires fresh information and re-dedication of your energy, attention, and skill. The first thing you need is a good **strategy**, a battle plan! This plan has to be reasonable and within your ability to complete.

Your survival and success will depend on the quality of your preparation and your personal investment in carrying out your plan. As you work to survive and grow, you will need to reshape your thinking, as we discussed previously. The following steps will be helpful as you proceed.

1. Set positive goals, short- and long-term.
2. Test your objectives; can they be achieved?
3. Check out the risks; be painfully honest.
4. Review your decision; is it really worth it?
5. Define the steps required; be realistic.
6. Think it all through; leave nothing out.
7. Consider what's needed from start to finish.
8. Develop a reasonable timetable.
9. Collect your resources.
10. Set your priorities and begin with Number 1.
11. Follow through – one step at a time.
12. Be patient and flexible; adapt as needed.
13. Give yourself credit as you achieve each step.
14. Celebrate your advances, and hang in there!

Caution: the Number One trap we all fall into is trying to achieve our long-term goals without dealing with our immediate needs first! We want to achieve too much too soon, so we try to jump ahead, skipping the steps needed here and now. This will defeat our plans, resulting in a lot of frustration and feelings of failure. **Success requires the discipline to do what needs to be done at the right time and in the right way.**

When you get discouraged, review how far you've already come. Sure there's still a lot left to do, but give yourself credit for the progress you've made. Then take a deep breath and take the next step.

Balance Your Growth

As you work toward a better future, you will find some aspects of yourself which only you can explore and develop. By giving attention and energy to each, you grow in many rich and rewarding ways. Think of each aspect as an essential part of who you are. No one of these factors is enough in itself, so don't focus on just one or two that you enjoy or are good at. The goal is to become a "complete" person by blending and balancing them all.

Becoming a complete person demands work in the following areas. As you develop your plan and strive to better govern your life, you must balance the effort you put into each. You may need to concentrate on a particular area for a while to achieve an immediate goal, but don't let any one area consume your whole attention. *"Take many small bites and chew slowly."*

1. Spiritual Growth

"Only by seeking satisfaction and peace within ourselves can we take power from our captors and make it our own."

Nothing is more essential to our growth than our relationship with our deeper nature and the universe beyond our physical awareness. Spiritual development helps us find the meaning and purpose of our efforts. It develops our inner resources for dealing with problems, gives us a central point of balance, and helps us identify the path which brings the most positive results for ourselves and those around us.

The more aware we are of our spiritual nature, the more progress we will make toward becoming a full and useful person. To strengthen our connection with the mystery and wonder of the universe, we must look **within**. By this I do not mean a retreat from reality, blind surrender to an all-consuming belief system, or escape into mental illness. Rather, each person must look deeply within themselves and within the teachings of any particular religion or philosophy for the path which best leads them toward spiritual advancement.

There are many widely accepted religions and spiritual teachings one can follow to develop his or her spiritual nature. And because this is the most private part of every person, it is not my place to tell anyone what to believe. My point is that development as a balanced person involves spiritual awareness and growth. This critical fact cannot be ignored!

Most religions and spiritual practices offer techniques – such as prayer, meditation, and rituals which celebrate their beliefs – to help people develop spiritual awareness and come into greater harmony with the universe. You can seek guidance from teachers, ministers, or often just "good people." And regardless of which religion or belief system you follow, you may also wish to learn more about **meditation**.

Meditation is an ancient technique used by many religions and belief systems to promote mental and spiritual development. There are many different methods. Some teach you to concentrate or focus your mind, while others teach you to free your mind in order to reach beyond your thoughts and get in touch with your spiritual essence. Through this process, you expand your connection with the Universe and internal peace of mind.

One advantage of practicing meditation is that it is something you can do anywhere at any time, without any special equipment, to advance in your spiritual beliefs and peace of mind. This makes it ideal for prisoners who have limits on their resources and physical liberty.

I strongly encourage you to **practice daily meditation** as a part of your spiritual development. As with learning to play the piano, dedication and practice are the secrets to success. Even five minutes of slow breathing and relaxation yields a major improvement in your mental and physical well being. There are many good techniques, some from Oriental and Mid-Eastern belief systems, such as Buddhism and Hinduism, as well as forms of meditation used by Christians and members of other Western religions. It doesn't have to be complicated: **just focus on your breathing!**

No matter what your religious background, you will find meditation concepts and techniques to be simple and of untold value. Find or develop a method that works for you and **stick with it**. You can refer to **Additional Resources** at the end of this book for more in-depth information on how to get started.

2. Mental Development

"Treat any brain cells you have left like long-lost friends!"

Your mind is your greatest single tool for achieving and sustaining freedom. Before you can begin to be free, you must be mentally clear and honest with yourself, prepared to recognize and cope with reality. Then you can use your mental focus to improve your education, health, job potential, or anything else. No matter how smart you are, you have only been exposed to a tiny fraction of the vast world of knowledge and skills. Now you have the time to expand your information and understanding. Make use of it!

As you know, positive opportunities are scarce in prison, so take advantage of whatever is available. Read, take academic classes, learn a craft – anything you can find to increase your knowledge and skills. Above all, find time when you can just **think**, to review and make sense of what you are learning.

Of all the areas of mental growth, none is more important than learning to control what goes on inside your head! What happens in your mind determines how you feel about and react to everything and everyone around you. If you act on your feelings without understanding them or their results, they may lead you into choices based on a mood of the moment rather than sound judgment.

A skilled warrior cannot afford to be swayed by fleeting emotional whims! You must master your emotions and the resulting actions. The best guide is direct experience. First, watch how your mind and emotions work and how you make decisions. This provides a chance to identify your values and figure out why you think the way you do. Next, observe what actions come from your thoughts and how they affect you and others. Are the results of your behavior pleasant, rewarding, and peaceful? Or do they produce pain, distress, and agitation? Are you making progress in exiting the maze, or are you just getting more and more lost?

When you understand the causes and the effects of your choices, you can exercise more control over your actions and choose to redirect your energy toward more positive results. You can use this same process of observation to decide if information and suggestions from other people are accurate and helpful. A big part of growing from a child to an adult is learning to tell who's right and what's real, then adapting to the new information.

As you work to improve your mind, seek advice from people whose experience, wisdom, and insight can assist your development. These teachers can help you learn to understand and apply the knowledge you are gaining. Good teachers cannot be judged by what they look like but by what they **know and do**. Don't expect them to be perfect, wear white robes, and float into the room. They are just people who know useful things you can benefit from. In fact, insight often comes in tiny bits from those we least expect as we interact every day.

You may also benefit from studying the teachings of such leaders such as the Buddha, Confucius, the Dalai Lama, Gandhi, Jesus, Malcolm X, Marcus Aurelius, Mohammed, Thomas Aquinas, and many others. Often the right thought at the right time helps us break through to a higher level of understanding. Therefore, we must keep our minds and hearts open to wisdom and guidance, no matter what the source!

Remain aware that your mind is your most powerful tool in the quest for true freedom and a rich, full life. As long as you live, you can continue to develop your understanding and improve the way you think and respond to yourself, to others, and to life itself. By making steady progress in these areas, you can achieve deep wisdom and peace...both in prison and in facing the challenges of the free world.

3. Physical Development

"If you wear out your body, where are you going to live?"

Clearly, if you ignore your body, it will become weak and unhealthy. On the other hand, the better you respect and care for it, the more energy you have to deal with all aspects of life and yourself. When your body is strong and stable, it acts as a basis for what you do mentally and spiritually.

Although we may not be able to avoid all diseases and accidents, there are two basic factors in physical health where we **can** take control: our diet and exercise. So consider these basic truths about the body.

1. You are what you eat.
2. If you don't use it, you lose it. (So exercise!)

First, let's look at what we put in our mouths. One key to good health is to limit the amount of fat, especially saturated and trans fats, and cholesterol. These are found in meat and dairy products and in many other foods as well. Trans fats have been used in processed foods such as snacks and store-bought baked goods, but are used less now because they are so unhealthy.

Most Americans consume about 35-40% of their diet as fat. Why? Because it tastes good. But to be healthy, we should have no more than 20-35% of the diet as fat, with less than half of that as saturated fat. We need some fat in our diet, but poly-unsaturated or mono-unsaturated fats are healthier. Trans fats are not a natural part of the diet; avoid them as much as possible.

Eating too much fat and cholesterol makes us overweight, clogs up our arteries, and causes serious problems. So cut down on fat. Eat less red meat and high-fat dairy products, eat more fish and chicken (without skin), drink skim milk, and stay away from fried foods when you can.

The number of calories we take in is another key to a good diet. Calories measure the amount of energy in food. We need the energy, but extra calories make us overweight. And most of the calories in our diet come from fat and sugar. Sugar gives us quick energy and tastes great, but it burns up fast, too. In fact, for a lot of people, sugar is the drug of choice. It gives them a pumped-up high, distracts them from their problems, and when the crash comes, they can just pop another Hershey bar.

Sugar is high-octane fuel, but it doesn't provide the raw materials to build and maintain a healthy body. For that we need protein and complex carbohydrates. Don't think that eating a lot of white bread will take care of this; our body turns refined flour into sugar. So to get healthy, cut way down on sweets and refined carbohydrates (sugar, candy, white flour, honey, etc.) Eat more complex carbohydrates (whole grains, potatoes, fruits, and vegetables). And when you buy packaged food from the commissary, read the nutrition labels; what you see may be scary.

A big source of sugar in our diet is from sweetened drinks. We drink sodas, tea, coffee, etc., but rarely drink water. The result: our bodies don't function the way they should and the sugar helps make us fat. And we often get a high dose of caffeine, a stimulant drug. Our body's chemistry depends on having enough water in our system–just water, not a combination of drugs and artificial flavorings. To be healthy, you need to drink two quarts of water a day. Cut down on soft drinks, diet drinks, and caffeinated drinks like tea, coffee, and many sodas. If you want to be healthy, **do it.**

Many of the things we take into our bodies aren't food. We can get hooked on lots of substances that help us pass the time or forget problems, but they definitely aren't good for our bodies or our minds. So give yourself a break: get help to give up smoking, dipping, alcohol, and other addictive drugs. We will discuss recovery from addiction more fully a little later in the section on **Recovery**.

Also look at **how** you eat. If you stuff yourself at every meal, you will get too many calories. Learn to eat till you're satisfied, then stop. You don't have to clean your plate or finish the bag of cookies at one sitting. There's no sense in skipping a meal to make up for overeating; this will just make you hungrier the next time you eat. Use low-fat foods like fruits and vegetables to fill up before you get to the fats and sweets. And eat slowly; this will help you digest your food better and give your stomach time to realize it's full. You can also drink a glass of water 15–20 minutes before a meal since it takes about that long for the stomach to feel full.

Next let's look at **exercise**. We used to exercise only to build stronger muscles and burn up excess calories. Now we know that exercise has many other powerful benefits, such as:

- Giving you more energy.
- Improving your endurance.
- Maintaining muscles, not flab.
- Increasing the blood chemicals that burn fat.
- Making you feel good by releasing chemicals called endorphins in the brain (a natural high).
- Reducing stress.
- Building self-respect.
- Helping you think more clearly and be more positive

So **just keep moving**; it will really improve your health and sense of well-being. Keep one thing in mind: it's not an all-or-none situation. You cannot change a lifetime of bad habits overnight. And I never said it was going to be easy! Changing your diet and increasing your exercise will take some time. As a prisoner, you can't always control these parts of your life. But you can have some control, such as taking a smaller portion, choosing not to eat some of the less healthy choices, deciding not to pig out on junk foods from the commissary, and working out in your cell..

Become more **aware** of your health needs and change what you can when you can. It is up to *you* to decide what you want and what you're willing to do to feel better and live a richer, fuller, healthier life. Changing your eating and exercise habits is a small price to pay to feel good. Get started **today!** It's worth it. And the more you work at it, the easier it will become. You will notice greater overall stability, less depression and anxiety, a more positive outlook, reduced hostility, and increased self-confidence. **You'll feel better,** and that is a real treat, inside a prison or on the streets.

4. Educational Advancement

"You can't dance the Rumba if you don't know the steps!"

As a social outcast, you know what it means to be "powerless." This is clearly not a desirable position to be in. So when you see **any** chance to improve your ability to function, jump up and grab it. There is no better way to do this than by improving your education. The better your education, on all levels, the more you have to draw from as you face the trials and opportunities of life. And the better you can compete in this competitive society.

Basic skills – reading, writing, and arithmetic – are essential for employment and just for daily living. You may never be a rocket scientist and you may not need a college degree, but you can certainly learn the basics needed to hold a job and understand what is going on in the world around you. If you don't have a high school diploma, you should definitely work to get your GED (high school equivalency diploma). This is something employers look for when screening job applicants. Plus, it is an accomplishment to be proud of.

Don't feel turned off by formal education just because you didn't do well in school when you were younger. As an adult, it's an all-new game! People learn in different ways, so you may need a different teaching approach to help you expand your education. You can work on things that interest you and proceed at your own pace. And don't be embarrassed about the things you haven't learned yet. What really counts is how much you are willing to learn to expand your view of yourself and the world. So fight your way out of anger and depression, find out what's happening, and get into something interesting and useful. Use each and every moment of your life to improve your mind and skills!

Almost all prisons offer some type of educational program; some provide basic education, while in others you can take college classes. Check with your education department to find out what's offered. If what you want isn't available, try studying what is available. For a prisoner, **any** positive activity is better than nothing. If your education goes beyond the courses provided, you might get a chance to tutor another student; many times teaching is the most powerful form of learning. If there is no education program at all, there may be a staff person or another inmate who would be willing to act as your tutor.

Often inmates are interested in taking online, distance learning, or correspondence courses. Many of these programs are high quality, but be sure you check on their reputation before you enroll. If you want to use credit from a correspondence course toward a degree, you need to confirm that other schools will accept those hours. Find out what the facility you're in will permit and look for a staff member to act as your "sponsor" to iron out any problems that come up.

Although basic education programs are often free to prisoners, there is usually a charge for college courses. This can be a real problem for many indigent inmates, but help may be available. Ask your education department about any free courses or financial aid you might be eligible for. This advice also applies to educational opportunities after release: financial aid is often available, and the school you want to attend should be your best source of information about it. Write to their counseling department for full information and forms. Don't let money stand in the way of your educational progress.

5. Vocational Development

"Just watching your fingernails grow is NOT a marketable skill!"

In order to take control and make progress in your life, you need a **burning desire**, the **skills** necessary to make your desire real, the **opportunity** to apply your skills, and **support** from those who can test your plans and assist your efforts.

You won't get anywhere without some job skills: special abilities that allow you to do something useful and earn a living. The ability to work to support yourself has a powerful impact on your survival, self-worth, and sense of achievement. These issues are essential for those branded as "outlaws" and are vital to your re-birth after prison.

The goal is to get real good at something people pay money for. So look around, find out what's happening that will help you increase your skills, and join in. It doesn't have to be something you want to do for the rest of your life. Every useful skill will increase your ability to function. Even more important than the skill itself is the **process of growth** it brings with it!

Inquire about any classes or training you can take in the facility. A lot of times you can find a teacher or counselor who will appreciate your initiative and help you. Your options may be very limited, but you don't know if you don't try.

If you can get into a trade (for example, welding or sheet metal work) while you are locked up, you can often continue or improve your skills after release. You could try drafting, auto body work, refrigeration repair, accounting, computer science, inventory control, construction...all are worth learning! Training programs in prisons don't prepare you completely for a job in that field, but any of them is better than nothing. One thing for sure: expanding your range of skills always pays off down the road.

Another area that needs your attention is how to find a job so you can put your skills to work. This is hard for anyone, but it will be a special challenge for someone with a criminal record – and a bad attitude will make it even harder.

Remember: preparation is vital to success. My self-help book, *Man, I Need a Job!*, and several other recommended resources at the end of this book (pages 129-136) discuss this issue in depth and offer practical advice on job hunting and overcoming a criminal record. I encourage you to obtain and study these resources when you are within six months of release.

6. Social Growth

"How well you deal with others depends directly on how you deal with yourself!"

Humans are social creatures; interacting with others is a big part of our lives. Think of yourself as one tiny fish in a great big ocean. Alone, you have little power and few resources; it's easy to get eaten by the bigger fish. To survive and prosper, you must learn to swim with the sharks rather than be their dinner. So building good ties with your fellow beings is more than just "good business"; it is essential!

As John Donne said, **"No man is an island."** To be healthy and whole, we need to learn to see ourselves as connected to other people. We can gain great satisfaction from a sense of closeness to others and a sense of belonging to the family of human-kind. The more we grow to view others as "sisters and brothers," the more we can understand about them **and** ourselves and the more we can share ideas, feelings, and growth. Such a sense of brotherhood is the natural and right way for humans to interact with one another.

But there is a Catch 22 here! We know we need a sense of closeness to help us feel kin-ship with others. But a prisoner lives with fear, hate, and suspicion of the world around. These negative emotions lead to extreme isolation. In this state of mind, any relationships based on trust, kindness, and compassion are sentenced to a slow but steady death.

Caution: Isolation is one of the most dangerous traps in the maze! If you stop and look at it, what greater damage can the experience do than to cut you off from partnership with yourself and with others? By closing your mind and heart, you are in effect exiling yourself to the Island of Despair.

The answer is to find a balance point between too much and too little. While we need a sense of connection with others, each of us will continue to be a separate in-dividual with our own ideas and desires. **Beware of extremes.** Dealing with people doesn't have to be all or nothing. For example, when starting a new relationship, we can find a middle ground – somewhere between immediate, total surrender and building an impassable wall between ourselves and other people.

As you know, it is wise to be careful and selective about whom we deal with and how we interact. For example, a person "shares" different things with a parole officer, a lover, an employer, a minister, a reporter, or a stranger. In every case, it is best to be conservative and develop your relationships slowly based on proven trust. In this way you are not leaving yourself open to hurt, but you **are** still open to exchanging energy and concern with others. The goal in social dealings is to respond to another person in the way that is most appropriate for your relationship and, at the same time, most beneficial for you and the other person.

7. Personal Ties

"Relationships are good when they benefit the well-being of all involved."

In order to hold onto some measure of humanity, most prisoners turn to their "peo-ple" – those few, if any, who still care if you live or die. Family and friends can become the lifeline to the world, to staying human, to emotional safety, often to hope itself. However, pre-prison relationships change as you and the people you care about adjust to the many burdens of prison life. And these relationships will change yet again upon release. Some of the changes are very dramatic. As a result, people relate to one another in some strange, intense, and frightening ways. The relationships most often experienced by inmates – and their most common pitfalls – are:

- **Committed relationships, which take many forms.** One of which is known as marriage. The institution of marriage is in major social and legal change, and I will not get into that here. What matters is that people often hold onto past relationships for stability… a sort of emotional life raft, while trying to build a future based on well-intended illusion. If either or both parties run out of gas, the union can die a painful death and result in "divorce." This is not anyone's fault, but a natural response to a very unnatural condition. People who were bound together on the streets must find new ways to stay connected, even if it means redefining their roles and expectations.

- **Jailhouse affairs:** Another type of relationship originates during the period of imprisonment whereby a prisoner hooks up with a free world person or even an available inmate. While intentions may be sincere, such connections quickly get lost in fairy tales and ten-page letters filled with fantasies. This type of personal involvement is a dangerous trap because there is nothing real to stand on when the day of release comes. All hell breaks loose as the parties try to live up to all that soap opera stuff once the initial circumstances of their relationship changes.

- **Free World Parent /Inmate Child:** The relationship between parent and child shifts radically from previous patterns but tends to endure better than other relationships. However, some family members may get fed up and turn away, leaving someone else (often the mother) to carry the load. This person may need special help to endure, and the whole family may become bitter and divided over the issue of loyalty to the prisoner.

- **Inmate Parent/Free World Child:** It requires special concern and understanding for a parent in prison to support the growth of his or her children. The child may feel abandoned, fear for the parent's safety, resent authority, do poorly in school, and have many behavior problems. Plus there will be a new set of adjustments to make when the parent is released.

- **Other Family and Friends:** These relationships come and go, depending on how tight the ties are with each individual. Some family members and friends hang in there; others cut you loose like you're ugly and stupid…or they just get tired of the steady effort of letters and visits. It's especially hard for friends to stay close when prisoners go through periods of bitterness and depression.

In every case, changes are so radical that new rules are needed in order to keep the relationship alive. Under these insane conditions, the best way to cope is to work together to re-define and re-direct the ways you deal with one another. You must create a brand-new relationship built on respect and honest concern. Throw out the past, get down to basics, and transform all your relationships into **true friendship**.

Friendship can occur on many different levels, from someone we see once in a while, to a good long-time buddy, all the way to our closest and most intimate companion. Friendship doesn't necessarily include the passion and intensity we associate with "love," but friendship must be the basis for any loving relationship that lasts over time and is good for both of the partners.

A good loving relationship is one of the most growth-producing experiences a person can have. It is based on a firm foundation of sincere commitment. Although we usually think of romantic love when we say loving relationship, the relationship between family members, such as parent and child, and between some close friends can also be deeply intimate.

Simply caring strongly about someone, wanting to be together, and wanting that person to care about you is not enough to establish an intimate loving relationship. Love is not just feeling; action is also required. No matter how much you care about someone, if your actions are harmful to him or her or block his/her attempts to grow, then you are not truly sharing love.

Therefore, let's review what goes into building a loving relationship that is good for the people in it, providing them valuable closeness along with room to grow. Research has found that the following elements are signs of a positive intimate relationship:

1. **Liking, acceptance, and respect** – Loving partners and friends really enjoy and think highly of each other. They accept each other as they are, even when one makes a mistake. They encourage toward positive goals, rather than nag or criticize. They care about one another's well-being without feeling that they have to control the other person.

2. **Ability to share deep inner feelings** – Partners know it is safe to talk about their most personal feelings, no matter what kind – anger, fear, joy, resentment, or caring. Their feelings are acknowledged as being real, even if the other does not agree. The friends accept responsibility for their own feelings, rather than claiming that the other person is responsible for how they feel.

3. **Honest communication** – Partners are willing to tell each other honestly how they feel about any topic. There are no issues that are hidden, off limits, or too scary to discuss. They talk to each other, not about each other.

4. **Balance of closeness and individualism** – Partners respect and encourage each other's differences, without losing their sense of togetherness. No one assumes that they know how the other person feels; each is responsible for knowing and expressing his or her own needs and feelings. The partners are interdependent – they help and support each other, but do not depend on each other as the center of their existence.

5. Fair balance of power and decision making – Partners share power and make decisions together, rather than competing to control the relationship. If there is disagreement, they negotiate until they find a compromise.

6. Effective problem solving – Partners are willing to admit when they have problems and to work together to solve them. They don't waste time trying to cover up the problem or blame it on each other.

7. Shared interests and values – Partners have a core of beliefs, values, commitments, and goals that they hold in common, even while they respect individual differences. They enjoy doing things together.

8. Flexibility and ability to change – Partners have common goals, routines, etc., but they are not rigid. They can agree to change plans and head in a different direction without too much stress or discomfort. Their relationship is not tied to any specific set of circumstances or patterns of behavior.

9. Openness – Partners feel comfortable doing things alone or with other people and inviting others into their home and activities. They do not depend on their relationship to meet all of their emotional needs and do not expect each other to give up all outside interests.

In conclusion, a loving relationship is a special and advanced form of friendship. It creates a positive bond between people built on honesty, respect, concern, and common goals. As with the construction of a fine building, the construction of a friendship takes patience, consistency, and determination. Of course, working to build a fresh, healthy relationship will in itself create a lot of stress, so proceed with caution. There are no magic buttons you can push.

One essential ingredient for building friendship is good communication: honesty and openness in expressing how you feel and a sincere willingness to listen when your friend shares feelings with you. Everyone involved must have a strong commitment to the relationship. Otherwise, you won't be willing to spend the time and hard work it will take to make your relationship better. Remember: the main building blocks will be honesty, commitment, communication, and a positive, caring attitude.

8. Recovery

"Recovery is living in BALANCE with yourself and the world around you!"

From birth to death we face suffering and distress. This is a normal part of being alive. On top of that, we often cause even greater injury to ourselves by our own choices and behavior.

To cope, many of us have developed behaviors to help us feel better or avoid pain. Unfortunately, some of these ways of thinking and acting make our old problems worse, plus causing new problems we never expected. We end up needing more and more of the "relief" just to stay even, until it becomes an addiction and we lose our ability to control it.

These destructive cycles of behavior (addictions) do great damage, robbing us of self-respect and a quality life. By giving something or someone control over our welfare, we set ourselves up for abuse. Surely being in the criminal justice system teaches us that! If we have abandoned control of ourselves to some chemical, person, feeling, concept, or behavior, **now** is the time to move beyond our addictions. This process of positive change is what we call "recovery." Only through constructive change can we bring joy and balance back into our lives.

The need for recovery is equally great for anyone who has lived through a lot of suffering – whether it came from others or ourselves, from addictions or depression, anger, fear, bad relationships, isolation, prison experiences, or false expectations of ourselves and the world. No matter what the source, most of us carry ten car loads of scars, pain, and emotional garbage that have collected over time. **Now our goal must be to heal.**

The first step toward recovery is to overcome denial and admit that you have a problem. Recovery, like any form of growth, requires commitment and hard, hard work. No one can or should do it for you. If you don't think you're ready to pay the price, look at the damage you are suffering by not working toward recovery. As long as you're weighed down by past suffering or controlled by addictive behavior, you can never be truly free. Never! So accept it as your responsibility to grow beyond the pain of the past and invest in a positive future. You owe this much to yourself.

Since recovery is such a demanding process, everyone needs help along the way. Many wounds are so deep and serious that you just cannot fix them all by yourself. Even Superman needed help when overcome by Kryptonite poisoning. There are many forms of help for recovery in the community: Twelve-Step and other self-help programs, counselors, treatment centers, health departments, hospitals, ministers, friends, and so on.

For prisoners, the choices are much more limited, but even then some kind of help is usually available. Learn to take care of yourself by reaching out for what you need to become a whole person. You can find more information about recovery and finding the right help in the self-help book *Life Without a Crutch* (see pages 129-136).

While it's totally okay to seek help, the last thing you want to do is transfer your needs and dependent behavior to yet another person or thing! **Stay alert:** no matter what your current status, the final goal is true freedom. The better you can control your own fate, the better you will feel about everything, especially yourself. The goal is to become your own best friend, to develop your dignity and self-respect. **You** are the foundation of your life and future, no one and nothing else.

9. Cultural Enrichment

"Knowing your roots helps set the foundation for your future."

You may think of "culture" as going to a dull play or trying to stay awake through an opera. If so, please reconsider. The cultural development I'm talking about is essential to the overall quality of human life. Exploring our culture means developing an understanding of our roots – going back to look at the paths people have followed throughout time and the lessons we have learned. Different societies have unique customs, art, ways of seeing the world and their place in it. Rather than just social or political history, I'm referring to **all** beliefs and efforts humans have used to make life deeper, richer, and more rewarding.

While being in prison sets you aside from the mainstream of society, it need not cut you off from the rich store of thought and knowledge we have collected over thousands of years. The best of human qualities are captured in art, science, music, literature, poetry, philosophy, religious and creative thought, and so on. No matter what the length of your sentence, you need to be in touch with energy and events from across the world. So reach out. Let your mind expand far beyond the limits of concrete and steel.

Suggestions: Use the prison library when and if you can. Read a newspaper to keep up with local and world affairs. Seek out free publications and subscriptions. Have your people send you books on a variety of topics such as art, different spiritual practices, poetry, geography, ancient history, anthropology, agriculture, or philosophy.

If you really want to put your time to good use, make an in-depth study of a specific subject, for instance, electronics, a period in history, or cosmology. Or study a foreign country you may want to visit one day; research its customs, history, and current political status. You can even study the language so you will be able to get around and enjoy your travels.

Rather than waste your money on junk from the store, buy a subscription to a publication such as *National Geographic, The New Yorker, Popular Mechanics, Time,* or whatever excites and expands your cultural horizons. If nothing else, read sections of the library's encyclopedia – anything that helps open your mind!

10. Recreation

"All work and no play makes you a mighty dull dude!"

The whole trip through the maze is so heavy we tend to focus only on day-to-day survival. This can make life total drudgery. It can sour our outlook on everything and lock us into a cycle of internal misery. We often forget how to laugh and have a good time, although this is essential to our physical and mental health. In truth, one part of growth is play! And it cannot be ignored.

Break out of your depression, get moving, be creative! Go out and play baseball or handball, work on hobby crafts, play checkers, take walks, read entertaining books, watch cartoons – just for the sheer fun of it! This doesn't discount the dreary nature of a cage or the burdens of reconstruction, but you can't afford to get lost in those. No matter how sad your situation, schedule some time every day to lighten up. It doesn't mean you like where you are, only that you have what it takes to adapt and survive.

Such efforts are necessary to keep your stress and attitude under control, both in the joint and with your loved ones. If you build some good "play habits" now, you will find they have a major influence on how well you adjust after release. Having interests to pursue just for fun helps make you a balanced person, as much as any of the issues mentioned above. Allowing yourself this joy in your life becomes your own private reward for taking care of business and doing a good job. It rounds out who you are.

More Than Survival

"Just remember, bud, if it can get this bad, it can get this good!"

Life in the system is often an endless series of efforts to cope with soul-bending boredom, interrupted only by moments of crisis. For many, the struggle becomes the focus of every thought and deed. People can get so consumed with the daily battle that they lose sight of the positive side of living.

When eaten up with efforts to survive, it's easy to forget there's anything else. You just keep yourself going with dreams of a better life. The danger is that future plans created in a cage are often just fairy tales you use to retain your hope and courage! When they fall apart, you face even greater failure and disappointment. These pitfalls create a powerful barrier to growth and building a better life.

To keep from getting lost, you have to remind yourself constantly that there is more to your life than punishment and pain. All your efforts have a positive purpose beyond just making it here and now. They are to prepare you for living a richer, fuller, more satisfying life!

The Bottom Line

Before we begin the journey through the "correctional experience," you need to wrap your mind around this fact: there is far **more** to being alive than your current plight in the criminal justice system! It may not seem that way to you right now. Depression and stress can make you lose sight of anything but the grief and madness of the moment. But of all the things necessary for growth, the most essential is **to maintain your hope of future good**.

It is essential that you keep your vision focused on the rewards for making it through the maze. So, just for the record, let's ask and answer some basic questions about the reality of the correctional ordeal and why you should bother to seek growth.

- **Will this nightmare ever end?**

    Yes, absolutely! One way or another, "this, too, shall pass." In most cases, it is not the end of the world.

- **What price has to be paid?**

    Honesty, courage, determination, and an absolute commitment to a better way. The best tools for pulling yourself out of the quicksand are hard work, good choices, patience, and consistency. You must be faithful to your potential as a human being and hold onto your appreciation of the beauty of life.

- **What steps are needed?**

    Establish positive short-term goals and procedures; maintain faith in long-term relief; and pursue growth on every possible level. Work to keep your mind free and your spirit strong. Above all, do not hesitate to seek help! Seek out the wisdom of mature teachers. Search until you find the knowledge, guidance, and support you need. Above all, never give up!

- **How long will it take?**

It takes as long as it takes! That may sound like jive but there is no other honest answer. Many time frames cannot be controlled or predicted, but others (such as the stages of post-release adjustment) **can** be influenced. You can't beat the game totally, but you can get ahead enough to both survive and grow. As your strength and focus increase, you will find you are slowly outgrowing the past. While still struggling to release yourself from your history, you will know, without question, that **it is** possible to become a balanced, healthy person! And every day of progress makes tomorrow a bit richer and more exciting, a bit more worth living. Even long-term captivity offers the potential for development of great insight and expansion of your character.

- **What is "success" for a felon?**

It is continued physical freedom, linked with steady progress as a positive, constructive human being. Success is not a fixed, final condition, but a state of constant **becoming**. Becoming proud, becoming healthy, becoming vital and free, becoming happy, becoming respected and secure, becoming comfortable, becoming honorable, **becoming more!** Although everyone would want to achieve this growth as a free citizen, the process can occur even through many years of imprisonment. For everyone, including prisoners, success is a condition of slow, steady growth and progress – developing more control, with ever expanding **dignity and pride**.

Success is not what you own but what you **are**. Not the worth of your car, house, or bank account, but the worth of your **word!** While others run around playing the fool, hurting themselves and others, you will be a true success because you insist on being a person of good heart and sound character. Face reality: success requires a total commitment while you are still down! It's not a promise you make to God in solitary or your mamma in a visiting room. It is an absolute commitment you make to **yourself!**

- **Can it be done, should it be done, and how?**

Without question, it **can** and **should** be done! The main difference between success and failure is a deep-seated commitment to be all that you can be! If there is any one secret to success, it is this: **you have to want it more than anything else in the world!** That means a steady investment of faith and effort. Only absolute dedication will take you far enough.

- **Is it worth it?**

Absolutely! But dealing with the problems a prisoner and family must face is tough. You may ask yourself, what's the use? Why bother? What you're experiencing is so intense that it often seems to overshadow everything else. You can keep your balance and faith by remembering that this is just one chapter in the book of your life; it is not the book itself!

Constantly re-focus your mind: true freedom is the goal! Not some silly fantasy or Hollywood image, but the real stuff. While others carry their own prison around with them in their heads and hearts, you have the choice of unlocking yourself just a bit more each day. And as you do, you will see more clearly that true freedom can only come from **inside** of you. This knowledge gives you the power to maintain hope and make good choices, both in the joint and in the streets. It is the first step to breaking the chains which bind you!

• Then what?

Is there anything on the other side of this sick, crazy trip?? You bet – functioning as an ever-more productive, creative human being. **The joys of being alive!** This is a rush worth living for, worth working for, worth the price of the ticket, no matter how long the journey or the sacrifices it demands! Be of clear mind and strong heart! And never, ever surrender!

3

Welcome to the Maze

"The challenge is to remain calm even as the bombs are falling."

AS WE BEGIN our journey through the insanity and sorrow of institutional life, stop and calmly reflect on the harsh realities of your situation. No matter how much experience you may have on the streets or in the system, you are now a "convict," under the power and control of a heartless process that doesn't care whether you live or die. No matter how slick, cool, or smooth you may be, you now exist at the bottom of the social sewer. You have essentially two options: **give up** or **get up**. Drown in the filth or learn to swim.

Be assured, your journey has a beginning and an end. The day of sentencing, the moment the gavel fell, represents the beginning...that's a done deal or you wouldn't be reading this. Now the concern is, how you can best cope with **today**, with each moment, as you move through this demanding experience.

Some will spend their last days in prison but most will not. And no matter how much time is required, **it is not the final goal**. An ex-con's ultimate purpose is to "get a life"! That means to achieve a rewarding level of comfort, accomplishment, and hope for a better future. This requires making positive, constructive use of every single heartbeat in one's determination to achieve pride, dignity, and quality of life, whether in a cage or on the streets.

For those who cannot see a light at the end of the tunnel, the situation is far more difficult than for short-timers because you've got to learn to make a home in hell. There are many types of hell in this world but each demands making the best of the hand we have been dealt. Each involves turning inward, taking refuge within your own mind, independent of the perversion and sadness all around you. The challenge, of course, is to make a home inside your own head without getting isolated and lost – to create a mental and spiritual garden where you can retreat into peace and beauty. We will discuss ways of handling this burden in the section "For Long-Termers and Lifers" (pages 68-71).

But no matter the length of your sentence or conditions of your captivity, in the face of such overwhelming adversity, how do you make the best of **right now**? This is a key concern we will now review.

The Trip From Arrest to Success

"Like French kissing a water moccasin, imprisonment leaves you breathless and damned relieved when it's over!"

When I caught my first bit at Angola (Louisiana State Penitentiary) in 1966 at the tender age of 23, an old con told me I was caught in a giant maze and no newcomer ever knew enough to escape it. *"Ace,"* he snickered, *"you'll get out when you've learned enough, and in your case that's gonna take a long time!"* Regrettably, he was right. And here I am, almost 50 years later, still struggling to understand and overcome what began as an act of blind, violent passion that ended up in a solitary cell.

Like most, I hit the joint frightened but determined to cope with whatever came down. I quickly found that even the most street-smart person in the world isn't ready for all the dark, sick jive that comes with being "Property of the State." Like all others I learned to survive, but there was no joy in living from hour to hour and count to count like a monkey in a cage.

So I did that bit and came home to a world I was no longer part of. A stranger in a strange land. There I found, as others have, that my insight only scratched the surface of what was required for a quality existence. Needing a new identity and source of income, I tried "dope dealer" on for size. And although I moved a lot of product, I had terrible taste in snitches, ending up back in federal and state joints in the mid-1970s. It was during this period I finally "got it" – **there has to be a better way!**

Since then, I've watched 50,000 or so cons and ex-cons struggle to find their way and have discovered how similar many problems and needs are. In fact, it is the predictable nature of the whole trip that makes this book possible. I have also learned that there is a **beginning** and an **end** to this wild race, with a whole bunch of vicious twists and turns in between. For someone lost in the heart of this maze, the list of potential traps is endless! So any reliable information you can pick up along the way is priceless.

Let me be upfront with you. If you've been out of the criminal justice system ten years, have a solid life and loving friends, a rewarding job and stable income, personal security, pride in your achievements, and peace of mind, you probably don't need this book. But, if you have achieved **anything less** than the above, be honest with yourself and be receptive to any new trick you can learn.

A Down and Dirty Tour

"Walk slow and drink a lot of water."

One purpose of this book is to reduce some of the traps and deadends a prisoner encounters time after time. With better vision, we can pursue truths that lead to final exit and life beyond this painful puzzle.

To do so, we're going to visit some major danger zones together, step-by-step, from arrest to recovery five years after release. The focus will **not** be on legal issues but the mental and social changes needed to survive and get ahead of this ugly game. This approach will be a **down and dirty** tour, with only minutes spent on what often takes years to experience. The aim is to provide an honest view that can improve chances of living through and beyond this dangerous journey.

You may be a "state-raised" character or some careless square who just fell off into the joint. Perhaps you are a loved one of a prisoner or simply a student in search of knowledge. You may know a little or you may know a lot about this path, but never think for a heartbeat that you know it **all**. No matter how hip, hard-core, or get-down you may be, this blueprint contains areas you have yet to explore and conquer! Why spend 25 years of hard knocks, panic, and pain just to discover insights you're already holding in your hands?

In addition, for their own well being, families and loved ones should give special note to the last chapter, Advice for Families of Offenders. Its useful insight will help them survive and grow beyond this painful period in their lives. This section also offers prisoners a helpful picture of what their people are faced with and what it takes for them to handle grief, fear, and depression. The more an inmate knows about the plight of their loved ones, the better he or she can support and encourage them during their times of critical need. **Never forget that it's a two-way street!**

This roadmap will help you rise above the limits of day-to-day survival by providing a "big picture. To tap its power, don't skip around – read it all. **Think** about it, step by step. Then go back, read it again and take notes, especially the parts you've yet to personally experience. Only in this way can you grasp the overall journey, rather than being lost in isolated events and concerns. If you reflect on what you learn here, you will come away with invaluable insight that enhances your well-being. Although this road often brings danger, damage, and dread, we will approach it as a learning experience and powerful opportunity for personal growth.

4

Waking Up in a Cage: Arrest to Conviction

You're Busted, Sucker!!

"Falling off into the criminal justice system is like being struck by lightning right on top of your poor old bald head!"

ARREST IS THE first step into the alien world of the American system of justice. It can be just a short-term hassle or the start of a long, painful journey that deeply affects someone's life for years to come.

It's a total shock to awaken in a jail cell, alone and confused in a world based on brute force, mind games, endless deceit, and frantic hopes for release. A family member or loved one is **equally** stunned by a prisoner's 3am call from a jail pleading for help.

An arrest upsets a person's balance and sense of security. It explodes patterns of living that you're used to. Immediately you snap to the fact that you are helpless and have no control over your freedom. Time seems to stop as your contact with the world is suddenly cut off.

The first concern is making bail, because there isn't much you can do to aid your case from inside a cage. So you reach out to **anyone** who will respond: to those few folks, if any, who care and will up your bond. Thus your arrest disrupts the lives of loved ones and friends who are called on to provide money and support.

It can also affect your relations with friends, your boss, school, and many others. The results of this abrupt event can pass in a matter of weeks or be the start of years of isolation and heartache. The longer someone walks this trail of tears, the more intense and far-reaching the effects.

Long Walk Off a Short Pier

*"Sick, helpless feelings come over you like a
storm cloud blotting out the sun."*

As you move deeper into the maze of police, lawyers, jails, courts, and prisons, some heavy social and mental changes occur. Without warning, things turn upside down and inside out. For both the "citizen accused" and loved ones, parts of daily life are severely disturbed.

To cope with the insanity of jail and the mystery of the courts, you frantically search for a "good" lawyer who will perform a legal miracle and remove this threat to your welfare. You lose lots of sleep over what the D.A. is going to do, what your probation or parole officer is going to do, what your mother or wife is going to do, what your lawyer is going to do, etc.

Your mind is filled with anxiety and dread. Should you cop out or go to trial, does your family still support you, can you handle the warfare inside a prison, will your girlfriend wait if you catch ten years, and so on. **nobody** wants to believe they are going to be found guilty or be sent to prison, and neither do the folks who care about them.

Here is where you learn that justice is often linked to the size of your wallet and that the lawyer you want is the one you cannot afford. Many folks end up with a court-appointed attorney, who is far too busy to talk with you until ten minutes before court. In the meantime, **everyone** hopes to slide with a probation or short sentence, but sometimes that doesn't work. There is **no** promise of sanity or reason in the extreme forces which command a person's fate at this point.

It's impossible to outguess the system: it's a brainless business that defies prediction. Things get so crazy and stressed out that many people end up plea bargaining just to end the immediate madness. In fact, many pressures are brought into play to drive you to cop a plea that will keep the wheels of justice rolling right along. For the accused and family, this is a time of hell on earth.

It is also a critical turning point that often ends in life-long damage and hard feelings. Many of the people who will read this book got done in right about here. Just before my hearing, my lawyer went into the men's room in the federal courthouse and shot up white china junk he'd scored with money he squeezed out of my mother. I guess he needed a fix of courage to plead me guilty for the max. "Justice" is a seven-letter word; so is "goodbye."

With One Fall of the Gavel

"Son, how old are you?" "23, your Honor."
"Just entering the prime of life ... and I'm going to take
seven years of it. Seven years hard labor,
Angola State Penitentiary. OK, next case."

Lost in a fog of confusion, the hour of sentencing arrives – a moment of shock and dismay for both the prisoner and loved ones. Standing before the judge, a few magic words and, bingo, you belong to the State. Even when you know what's coming down, you're too spaced out to grasp what's happening or how it will affect your future.

It all happens so quickly! The gavel falls and the deal is done. There is no going back. If your sentence results in jail time, probation, and/or a fine, you can usually cope with it without too much trouble. Jail time may be fairly short, and probation requirements are usually not too heavy: you must report, follow the rules, and pay your fees. It definitely can be tough, but if you keep your life together everything turns out okay. Probation officers spend 90% of their time on the 10% of their caseloads who just **insist** on going to the pen.

Many probationers feel very abused by the actions of the police and courts. It's human nature to promise **anything** to keep from going down – and then bitch and moan after the deal is cut. People often show their anger and distress by resisting their terms of probation. Some get so hostile they say to hell with it and fail to report. This can happen when people get depressed, short of funds, careless, lost in addiction, or sideways with their probation officer. Yet no matter how stressful probation can get, it is far better than going to the pen! To make it on probation, you need to stay cool and clean, keep your act tight, and meet your commitments. There will still be unexpected dangers, but if you are on top of your game, you have a good chance of success.

Sign Me Up!

"If you sign up and don't show up, lean way over and
kiss your sorry ass goodbye."

When push comes to shove, most people would rather be eaten by a shark than go to the joint. So they rush to sign up for any local program that will satisfy the judge and keep them out of prison. But this can be a real trap if it turns out to be a bumpy ride!

No matter what kind of program you join or get assigned to, it will have its rules and requirements that cut into your life, demanding your time, energy, and resources. Even more, your probation officer will expect to see **positive changes** in your attitude and actions. So just because you score work release, boot camp, drug treatment, electronic monitoring, sex therapy, family counseling, a halfway house, or whatever, you are not home free. Stay alert: if you drop the ball, the judge will slam dunk you!

You are at a point where you have an important chance to work your way out of the maze and avoid the much heavier changes down the road. The requirements may seem Mickey Mouse, but do yourself a favor and take them seriously. One thing for a probationer (and parolee as well) to keep in mind: about **half** of all people sent to the joint were under supervision on the streets but failed to comply with the contract they signed. In many cases, revocation comes from walking away from a program or just failing to report, even if you don't pick up a new felony.

So if you are sentenced to probation or put in a program as an alternative to prison, make the best of a bad situation. Keep your game tight and be very careful not to send **yourself** down the river. If you do, you'll end up chained to someone even uglier than you, on a bus that doesn't stop at the Dairy Queen.

Flushed and Forgotten

"The day you're sent to prison, listen for the sound of running water because you've just been flushed down the social toilet!"

If the sentence is to prison, **suddenly everything gets radical!** One minute a citizen with rights, the next just a slave with a number for a name. Now, by law, ownership of you is transferred to the State. If you want to do **anything** from now on, some stranger with a bad attitude has to give you permission.

In truth, this is one of the most dramatic and far-reaching moments a person can experience. It's odd how a process which takes only ten minutes in court can require ten years of supreme madness to deal with and another ten years of stress and hard work to recover from.

The prisoner and loved ones turn to the lawyer for guidance about an appeal, shock probation, boot camps, visiting hours, what can be taken to prison, how parole works, etc. But the lawyer is **long gone!** The family then turns to the prisoner for direction, but he or she doesn't know what's happening either. It's the blind leading the blind!

This new part of the journey may last a few months, 20 years, or even unto death; it often demands every last resource of a person's mind, body, and spirit. Indeed, every day can bring new problems and heartache. Few experiences in our culture present a greater demand for change or a more intense challenge for personal growth. As I was told, *"It's a short step down and a long step up."*

If sentenced to prison, especially for a long period, you cease to be part of the real world. You become a mere ghost that walks and talks, a faceless number. Overnight all contact with life as you know it – food, fashions, daily activities, **everything** – comes to a screeching halt. Once sentenced to the joint, you become a public zombie, physically alive but as socially dead as a door knob.

You have just bought your ticket to the maze. The door marked "IN" is lit in neon; you even get an armed escort to help you enter. But once inside, you are stone alone and there is no exit in sight. Your thoughts, feelings, dreams, ambitions, skills, and hopes suddenly cease to be important to **anyone** but you and those few who choose to stand by you. From this point on you will be constantly looking for a way out. But what appears to be an "Exit" often turns out to be only a door painted on a concrete wall!

Saying Goodbye

"It's hard to say a tender goodbye as you're being dragged away in 35 pounds of chain."

Sudden loss of physical freedom is shocking. But the hardest part is being cut off from those you love. In many cases everyone's attention has been focused on the plea bargaining or trial. All energy has been spent on the outcome of efforts in court. As a result, there is seldom any real chance to prepare emotionally for the impact of separation.

By now everyone is so blown away and things move so quickly that there may not be any real chance to say goodbye. This is especially true for children; they are deeply confused by the stress and excitement and are trying to deal with the fact that daddy or mommy has vanished. This places a heavy burden on the person who is caring for the kids, answering their questions, and filling the gap of the parent's absence.

If you are on the streets and know what's coming, call time-out a few days before you are to be sentenced or report to prison. If you can, it's good to spend some quiet, quality time with those you love, just being close and trying to calm down. It helps to build some happy, positive memories to fall back on later.

I don't know of any graceful or easy way to cope with tearful farewells. Everyone involved, prisoner and family, reflects on what they wish they had said and done when they still had the chance. If the separation was rude and abrupt, it is important that the prisoner get in touch with the family as soon as possible and assure them of his or her safety and well-being. There is no reason to burden them with horror stories or to unload a lot of emotional garbage on them which they have no way to remedy.

Now the whole nature of how people relate to each other changes. The day-to-day chance to talk, share, and touch comes to an abrupt end and new ways must be found. From now on, you must learn to express yourself in letters, cards, poems, art, and visits. Your contact becomes **indirect**, but you can learn to adjust and find creative ways to express your thoughts and feelings. For more insight into these changes, give special attention to "Advice for Families of Offenders" on pages 102-124.

I'm Gonna Appeal!

"Don't panic and base your future on an endless series of false hopes; stay calm as a clam and get the facts!"

A person just convicted almost automatically considers an appeal. This seems reasonable because the decisions of the court are considered "unfair." Yet fairness, in the sense of moral correctness or justice, has even less to do with the appeal than it did with the trial.

Before you do anything, **two** facts have to be dealt with. First, if you plead guilty, generally no pre-trial motions were made and little evidence was presented. Agreed pleas are not heard by a jury and involve no jury charge. Therefore, there is very little to appeal from a guilty plea. Guilty pleas are rarely set aside on appeal.

Second, appeals are not a chance to have someone else correct a sentence or make a "fair" ruling. Instead they are simply motions which tell a higher court that someone – judge, juror, or attorney – made a **big** mistake. An appeal is not a new trial. It is a **written request to review one or more specific legal decisions** made during the case. Only those trials where a big mistake was made will be reversed (when the Court of Appeals finds some error in the trial court's actions and orders a new trial or a dismissal).

More than nine out of ten appeals will be affirmed (left unchanged). In the meantime, the appellant (defendant who appeals the case) and his or her loved ones can become absorbed in a long, expensive (many years and many thousands of dollars) process that may only build false hopes.

Appeals take a long time, partly because so many are filed. The frivolous (worthless) ones stand in line with the good ones. The appellant spends valuable time and funds in a process that is unrewarding 90% of the time. So before you jump off into it, you need to take a close look at the appeals process and the facts of your case.

This requires a review of the transcripts (official record) of the trial. These are the first major expense, which can be over a thousand dollars even for a short trial (unless you qualify as indigent). Then you need a **qualified** appellate lawyer to closely review the proceedings to see if some major mistake was made in the process of the trial (usually requires a retainer, and much more if the lawyer decides to take the case). Remember, you must find a mistake in the **process**, not in the facts. If none exists, you have no basis for an appeal and that's that. Cold but true.

If you have a short sentence, it may not make sense to appeal because you may make parole or be released before the appeal is finally heard. But for someone with heavy time and serious trial errors, it may be real smart to learn some law and fight your case. There are a lot of jailhouse lawyers who will claim special insight into how to beat your case, but very few really know their business.

Like anything else, the quality of your efforts and preparation are critical. Be careful not to let your despair warp your judgment. If you're going to do it, spend the time and energy to do it right. Take things one step at a time, learn patience, and don't send your mother out to mortgage her home to fund some hopeless grasp for freedom.

5

Falling Off Into Hell: Life in Prison

Chained Down and Prison Bound

Stripped and Shipped

"I was no longer a 'free citizen,' just a social outcast exiled to a giant, government-run dumpster."

THEY ALWAYS PULL the chain before the birds get up, so you begin your day locked down inside a crowded, smelly old bus or hunched over in the back of some sheriff's van. Of all the trips a person takes during a lifetime, few if any have such a powerful outcome! While the traffic moving around you rushes toward work and school, you struggle with your chains, listen to the drum of the engine, and fight to control the knot of sick fear growing in your guts.

As the miles click by, an amazing mutation is taking place. You **know** something very heavy is happening but cannot grasp the nature and impact of it all. In fact, you are not moving from "point to point" like the rest of the traffic, but from one dimension of reality to another. Later in life you may try to explain to others the shift that occurred during those dawn hours, but only those who have made this unearthly journey will ever understand.

Like a snake shedding its skin, your identity starts to peel away. Rather than being a parent, student, or truck driver, the label of "**criminal**" begins to define you. Over the months and years to come, you will grow to identify with and adapt to your new role. From this day onward, your attitude toward yourself and the world will change, and so will the way you carry yourself. It's not unusual for **every** aspect of the way you think, feel, and behave to be touched by your new status.

By the time you finally arrive, all stiff and frantic, the early changes have already occurred. Whatever your social status when you got aboard, it now resides in the weeds along some blacktop highway. Every newcomer feels buck naked, like prime vulture bait. And from this heartbeat on, 90% of your time and energy is spent working to cover your ass. It is this **constant, urgent demand** to adapt or perish which draws you, against your will, into the Devil's Den.

Welcome to Hell

Going to prison is like being stuck in a recurring nightmare. Everything may seem the same, but in fact everything is different. What "appears" is often not what actually exists. Different values and rules are now in force. But forget the war stories; what's the bottom line? What is a prison **really** like? Not the walls, the bunks, and the bars, but the life lived inside?

I've heard it defined many ways. "A concrete graveyard," "a human outhouse," "a hate factory," just to name a few. In truth, prison is a huge pressure cooker filled with human pain and treachery, all mixed together and simmering on a slow fire of stress and fear. No matter what words you use to describe it, it is a place where people silently cry in their sleep and fight to hold onto their sanity and hope.

Prison is not **real** in the way things are on the streets. But it's such a hard, cold, painful illusion that it seems to be reality-for-sure! Actually it's a false image, **a cruel cartoon**. It doesn't run by the same rules as the world you've left or the one you'll return to. There is no "long-term" or "short-term" – there is only **right here**, **right now!**

Like a computer, what makes a prison work is its **operating system:** the way people and things are defined and set up to relate to one another. First, the Cons to the Man and the Man to the Cons. Then the Man to each other and the Cons to each other. And, last, how **everybody** handles their roles and business, day in and day out. When you learn how things really come down, you realize that **all** the players are acting out jive roles – roles which are totally opposite to successful life on the streets. And I mean **both** the rulers and the ruled! What really kicks your ass is when people you thought to be righteous flip, turning into liars, snitches and fools; you must always stay alert!

The Number One prison code is that "kindness is weakness." **Everyone** wears "a different face for every place" and preys on one another, with mental and/or physical backstabbing being a daily reality. **Quickly** a prisoner learns that it's your "friends" who can hurt you the most because they know your business. Only those close to you **know** where you keep your property and how to jack with your head when an important letter doesn't arrive.

Danger: this is a place where screwing with the minds and emotions of "gofers" is considered good sport. So, in the end, you cannot afford to have friends as they exist in the streets. You may go through a series of running buddies or folks you hang with, but **never** let anyone get close to your heart. This is tough because it keeps a person very alone and at odds with the whole concrete jungle, but no one can afford to broadcast their feelings in a snake pit.

You soon discover that prison is a phony, lonely place. It's **painfully easy** to get tricked or trapped into living by terror, pressure, and unending hustles. For many, it becomes a madhouse where nothing makes sense, a void where nothing matters but survival. One major step in survival is understanding the nature of **respect:** learning how to give it and how to get it. Respect is based on the size of your heart and how you carry yourself; it is not built on the size of your arms or mouth.

Dancing Through a Minefield

*"It's like stepping off into a mine field.
You never know when the next blast will come,
without warning, totally beyond your control."*

A prison is like a giant trash can occupied by 3,000 hungry, hostile cats **all** after one little fish bone! In order to survive, you must learn the rules and adapt in a hurry. If you don't, you perish.

There are no true signposts to reality in prison, so it's easy to get lost if you don't run a tight ship. Many people do their time lost in a fantasy world, placing faith in what they wish could be (like bogus writs, pending changes in the law, early release, another appeal, etc.) rather than what actually **is**. Also, many inmates and their loved ones get lost in the mindless jive of prison war and power games. This is deadly because each new day draws them deeper into the falsehood and deceit of prison life.

All too often there are no logical reasons for things that happen in prison. Life is a roller-coaster moving from one crisis to another, with sheer boredom filling in between the stops. Everyone who takes this trip – inmates and families alike – has to cope with a series of abrupt, absurd events. It's usually a waste of time to try to figure out what has come down or why. Most of the time it's better for an inmate and loved ones to focus on **damage control** rather than going into blind battle.

I admit that it is **very** hard not to react emotionally and violently when something "totally wrong" comes down. You want to stand up for yourself and release your anger and frustration. Such reactions are very human but ask yourself one question: *"Is this going to make things better for me or make things worse?"* If the answer comes back, *"Worse – but I don't give a damn,"* then you are playing right into the hands of the enemy. Stop. **Think.** And **refuse** to go for the bait!

Beware the Traps

*"It's an endless series of trapdoors. You never
know which one is going to drop open or when,
so you've always got to be on your toes."*

From the moment you enter the maze to the moment you leave, you must expect to deal with countless traps. Like a human computer game, each step deeper into the system presents a new set of dangers.

The good news is that you learn to cope by basing your reactions on smart mental choices rather than raw emotions. You must learn to survive and flow with what comes down around you. This involves two levels of skill. First, you must learn to control your mind and emotions, as previously discussed in "Reshape Your Thinking" (pages 19-21). The second is covered in the following chapters dealing with physical and practical adjustments. As you learn to merge **both** types of skills, your present and future welfare will continue to improve.

If you keep to yourself, think before you act, watch what's going on, stay alert, and keep your mouth shut, you can do your time without always being on someone's hit list. **note:** do **not** accept favors; the payback is often more than you can afford. Staying invisible is the best way to go!

Obviously, **anything** that makes you a target is uncool. The basic traps to avoid are drugs, gangs, sex, and gambling. I would include coping with the crazies and the fools in that list, but they come with the territory. You have to learn to be **political** and deal with the snitches and idiots as smoothly as possible.

Your fate is determined by how you carry yourself and deal with people! Ripoffs finally get ripped off. Con men end up getting chumped. What goes around comes around. Lots of people fall off into gangs in the joint for protection, dealing, status, etc. But it is usually a bitter trap! All it did for Jesse James was get him shot in the back by a cowardly "home boy." Even Jesus got done in by one of his tight men for a handful of silver. Watch those around you very carefully; if they will backstab someone else, they will sure as hell do it to you. So stay alert to reality! When your fate can be swayed by a bunch of self-serving predators, it's amazing how quickly you can become the next in line to be had.

To put it bluntly, this is not a make-believe game where you can call "King's X." It is a cold-blooded, full-time horror show where your decisions and actions **directly** impact your stark survival. Therefore, the **last** thing you want to do is to surrender control of yourself to a set of rules made by losers, liars, and mental midgets. That's the most honest way I know to put it.

No matter how careful you are, there's no guarantee that trouble won't find you from time to time. But life is a lot easier if you focus on reality and don't beat on your chest, run your head, or try to abuse those weaker than you. This is just smart business, because there will always be someone close at hand to do the same unto you.

Here are some basic rules to follow to help reduce the hassles:

- **Always** think before you act; afterwards is too late.
- Trust no one and be very cautious who, if anybody, you pick as friends: it's your "buds" who know when you take a nap.
- Live your life in prison, not in fantasies of the streets.
- Maintain your sexual dignity by any means necessary.
- Hope for the best but expect the worst.
- Obey the rules – no one said you have to like it.
- Never put your business on the street or wave any flags.
- Treat your loved ones like 24-karat gold.
- Ask your people for only what you need to **survive**. Make no demands, and try not to snivel too much.

- Get healthy and stay strong – physically, mentally, and emotionally.
- Do unto others **just the way** you want them to do unto you!
- Respect yourself – never surrender your mind, body, or soul.
- Refuse to engage in self-pity.
- Stay calm as a clam and patient as a saint.
- Be real – the only thing you run in prison is your head.
- Never try to beat a shark at his own game. Sharks never sleep.
- Hear no evil, **see** no evil, and, for your own sake, speak no evil!
- Don't accept favors, gamble, borrow money, or push drugs.
- Never play bad ass or King Kong; you will be killed.
- AIDS leaves no survivors; masturbate.
- The past is dead and stinking; move forward, never backward.
- Grow! Use your time to expand your knowledge and understanding.
- Avoid prison mind games! Do your time, don't let it do you!
- Don't try to pray your way out.
- Get and stay real with yourself – live on facts, not illusions.
- Figure out who put you in the joint: look in the mirror.
- Do your own time, quietly and with class.
- Prepare yourself for where you want to be three years after release.
- Help others when you can, but don't be a chump.
- Do square business – earn respect.
- Leave your anger in the joint when you walk out.
- Keep this book handy and review it every three months. Tell your people to get a copy; it will improve their understanding.

Reading the Signs

"Knowing when to duck is very valuable information!"

Adjusting to all these new "rules of the game" can be overwhelming. But there is one powerful secret that the Man never tells you and your mother doesn't know. **Everything** that happens to you is part of a **predictable** pattern. What you are feeling and living through has been repeated time and time again since the first U.S. jail opened in 1789. The boxes have different names, **but what goes on inside of them is all the same**.

As one isolated person, you feel helpless against the forces which confront you. It is natural to believe that what's coming down is unique to you and you alone. **Not so!** Millions of people from coast to coast were, are, or will be on the same path, felt the same feelings, and shared the same hopes as you are this moment! I promise you this is true.

So how does this help you? It is your first essential tool for survival and growth. It means that adjustment in **and** out of prison happens in some highly predictable stages, most of which can be forecast like a pending storm. In short, you can learn to prepare for events and your own reactions before they happen. You are **not** totally powerless and at the mercy of the situation!

Stay alert! Watch the changes that others go through; look for patterns in their actions and reactions. Become aware of the stages of your own changes and behavior. For the first 90 days you are numb with shock and confusion. During this time you're tested in a dozen different ways; you may have to go into physical battle to keep your dignity. No matter who you are, this is a hard period filled with distress.

After the initial shock come six to nine months of grief and depression from losing your freedom and family. Most people do tough time during this period and have to be very careful not to lose their balance. To make things worse, you must carry this burden in silence; if you "snivel," it is taken as a sign of weakness by others.

Some young first offenders are sent to rehab for a short sentence. In this case, you're busy from the moment you arrive. If you happen to get into a rehab program, even if it is lame, keep a low profile, follow the rules, and don't blow it.

However, most people who have been down before or who drive up with a heavy load do their time the old-fashioned way: sunrise to sunset behind brick walls, double fences, and rows of shiny razor wire. It takes about 12 to 24 months to really settle in and get a grip on yourself. By the third year you have a good handle on what's cooking throughout the joint. By the fifth year, you've "found a home." From then on it's a matter of keeping a handle on what you've been able to carve out for yourself. Be careful – folks get **very** protective of their turf!

While you are learning to cope with what's going on around you, another very important change takes place. You slowly adjust to the way time itself changes. A day in a cage is like a week in the free world, a week like a month, a month like a year, a year like a decade. And as for holidays, well, they are just another day – one less to do. Events seem to stretch out as daily life goes into slow motion! If you do three to five years or more, you will definitely notice the impact of this time shift during your first six months of life back on the streets!

All the changes you go through have deep and long-lasting effects both during and after captivity. Little by little, day by day, you adapt to the folly of a joint in order to handle it. As you become more and more cut off from **everything** you value, the warm, positive aspects of daily life slowly drift away. At the same time, you become more and more involved with the cut-throat values of prison life.

So stay aware! After a few years, contact with the real world slowly dies and memories grow dim. Then it's all too easy to get lost in the false, shallow trash that goes on 24 hours a day. After five to seven years of this, you can get so caught up in prison values that you become more of a **prisoner** than a **person**. At this point, you have become "institutionalized" – mentally more "in" than "out."

If this happens, it is because you have simply run out of gas; the joint has drawn off all your energy and hope. As a cell partner once put it, *"You can't see over the barbed wire anymore."* No matter how much time you are doing or under what conditions, you must not let this happen! The only time you're **really** beat is when you surrender your spirit to the falsehood and dishonor of a prison. Hold onto your self. And **never** lose sight of your need for constant growth as a human being.

Staying in Touch With the World

Misery Loves Company

"The world views you as they do atomic waste. If you have a faithful friend or devoted mother left, treat them like 24-karat gold. It's loving, it's right – and it's good business."

Prison is often referred to as a war zone. And in war, people must work to hold onto their humanity and the values that make life worth living. Most often we do this through our ties with family, loved ones, and friends. However, prison life can cause serious damage to our relationships with people in the free world.

FACT: Inmates are often very selfish, demanding a lot from their people. Partly this is because we are cut off from the world. As prisoners, our status is so harsh and remote that we have little to hold onto and many limits on what we can do for ourselves. So we tend to overwork those few who care. The most obvious way is for money: for store goods, visits, appeals lawyers, phone calls, a radio or fan for our cell, law books from the free world, support for children, new tennis shoes for the rec yard, etc.

Inmates are often equally thoughtless of their loved ones' limited time, energy, and emotional well-being. We act as though they have nothing else to do but react to our needs and requests. How dare they go on living day to day while we suffer in the joint! When we get ourselves into trouble, we tend to expect everyone around us to pay the price. Being in prison makes it easy to get lost in wishful thinking, self-pity, and false ideas, so let's set the record straight.

- **Fact One:** In many cases your people are poor, physically ill, and emotionally tired to the bone. They often try to keep this to themselves so as not to burden you. In fact there is damn little they can do, if anything. They are **not** miracle workers. And don't cop an attitude because they all get together for Christmas dinner and actually have a good time! Do **not** lay guilt trips on people for going to see a box office hit while you're stuck in an isolation cell.

- **Fact Two:** Your old lady is **not** sleeping with the National Guard! Just because you're scared and insecure, don't expect her to sit in a corner and cry till you get home. She needs your trust and day-to-day support to be well and strong. It's bad enough that you are a social zombie who comes alive only in loud visiting rooms, long letters, and sexual fantasies. Show her what true love is by being fair, honest, considerate, and trusting. This may not work; you might break up anyway. But I guarantee that you stand the best chance of keeping her if you are a true friend and concerned partner.

- **Fact Three:** Only in very rare cases did your people have **anything** to do with why you are in the pen. You are there because you got "loose and ludicrous," in one way or another. Even if it was a bum rap, it is still **your** bum rap. So in most cases your people are having to deal as best they can with a condition you and the State laid on them. In short, it's **your** load to carry. When you do need serious help, make sure what you ask for is fair and doable. Don't send your pregnant wife to see the judge or ask your blind mamma to put up her retirement money for your appeals lawyer. Come on!

- **Fact Four:** Loved ones are the only "safe" people on whom you can unload your feelings; this includes your fears, anger, war talk, anxiety, and distress. They are the only people you can afford to be human with. But what do you think it does to your mother's mind to tell her you want to kill your cell partner for stealing your groceries? It is understandable that you are upset, but cut her some slack! If you don't know how to handle the madness of your situation, what makes you think she does?

- **Fact Five:** As a "criminal" you don't have many friends left. And even they are two-thirds fed up with your status *and* long line of jive. Many inmates have burned their people really badly, left them hanging, and, after all this, can't understand why their folks don't trust and support them. So you want to walk real lightly with those few friends and loved ones who still care about you. Be careful not to get so angry and depressed you drive them off! And, last, don't take anything for granted: express your sincere appreciation for every positive effort and favor they do.

First Your Money...

"There's an old jailhouse saying: 'First your money, then your clothes, then your old lady/man goes.'"

No inmate in the world wants to hear that! It's bad enough being powerless, cut off from the community, and fighting for your survival without having to worry about losing your main squeeze. For most prisoners, the most important part of their personal life is that person dearest to their hearts.

Yet the loss of important personal ties in prison is a frequent and painful fact of life. It does no good to deny the reality of it or to sit around and be eaten up by fear and worry. It is **critical** to keep your mental and emotional balance!

We all have to live through deaths in the family, and they can take place on many levels. If your relation with someone dear to you hits the wall, you cannot afford to be overcome by grief and depression. If you're not real careful, your grief will come out in anger and violence, which usually makes your plight even worse. Never permit the agony that comes with loss of a loved one to blind you. **Beware: your position doesn't permit you to surrender to grief.**

To make things worse, we often make up a lot of stuff in our minds that just isn't true. This happens because we lose track of reality, get lost in self-pity, are overcome by fear, or at times just go totally insane. For example, a friendship that was only a passing thought on the streets becomes a flaming inferno right off a TV soap opera when you catch a fresh ten-year sentence! Why? Because you need something to hold onto. **But just because you need it doesn't make it real.** The problem with make-believe is the pain you get when reality kicks you dead in the middle of your chest! So don't set yourself up for more distress than you've already got. In the end, the hope and support you hunger for has to be found **within you**.

Even though it's a major relief to have somebody out there, what if he or she just cannot hang on? I'm not talking about a worthless person here, but one who is **simply overwhelmed**. Remember that prison and its effects on people are totally unnatural. There isn't any guaranteed way to keep a romance or marriage alive under such absurd conditions. Many try, and really give it their best shot, only to find it's just too crazy and painful to handle.

Inmates cope with this issue in different ways. Many prisoners try to direct or dominate the life of someone in the streets. They use pitiful stories, guilt trips, spiritual awakenings, romantic promises, vows of long overdue change, or even threats of bodily injury. This is mostly to give themselves the illusion of retaining some of the security and control they have lost as a prisoner. The person in the free world may even try to go along with the game, but no one can or should "possess" or rule another, especially from the third tier of a cell block.

The only **real and useful** way to build or maintain a personal bond from inside a prison is through honesty, respect, and true concern. In fact, this genuine caring is all that really works on the streets, too. Do yourself a big favor: forget the fantasy/romance trip, and focus totally on **true friendship!** It's the only way to keep love alive in the face of loneliness, midnight anxiety, holiday depression, fear of abandonment, the screaming hornies, visiting room heartache, and the endless forms of confusion, longing, and pain.

Building positive, rewarding friendships is an art in itself, a skill worth learning for life during and after the joint. While you have so much time to reflect on the way you do business, give special attention to the earlier section on "Personal Ties." When you stop and look at it, **everything** we do involves some kind of relationship. How well we can build and maintain ties between ourselves and the world has a very powerful impact on the quality of our lives.

Health Needs in the Jungle

Not Arrested, *Saved!*

---

*"Man, you weren't arrested, you were saved!
It was so cold up under those bridges they took
pity on you and locked you up!"*

A lot of prisoners come off the streets in sad shape due to self-abuse of one form or another (booze, drugs, and general loose living). You can always knock off the speed freaks and crack heads because they look like they can slip between the bars. People who were burning themselves up often say that if it hadn't been for getting busted, they would have ended up on a slab. In short, their lives and health were out of control.

So let's face it, very few prisoners were health nuts on the streets. About the only exercise most outlaws get is running from the cops or stumbling out of topless joints at closing time! When you're strung out or ripping and running, you tend to treat your body like a chemical waste site. Plus, pulling a trigger is a far cry from an aerobic exercise!

As a result, you fall into prison in poor shape. Needless to say, a pen is not a health resort waiting to make you fit and firm. But you **have** to re-build with what's there or be trampled underfoot. And let me stress that it **is** possible to gain good health while locked up. As bad as it all may be, countless people all over the world have learned to survive and prosper on far less than you have in most U.S. prisons.

Survival of the Fittest

---

*"A prison is a place where the vultures are always circling.
You don't want to be viewed as the next available carcass."*

When it comes to taking care of themselves, there are basically two kinds of people. Those who do and those who don't. It's easy to tell the difference. The ones who don't are usually fat, slow, sloppy, sick a lot, depressed, stressed out, lazy, moody, withdrawn, vulnerable, and down on themselves. And keep in mind that people who don't treat themselves with respect don't earn respect from anyone else.

A joint is **definitely** not a place to be weak and unhealthy! This doesn't mean you must be a gorilla to survive, but you sure don't want to be viewed as a broken down "lame." Everyone knows who can take care of themselves and who cannot. It's reasonable to say that the weak and unhealthy are on the bottom of the prison pecking order. Therefore, every prisoner needs to be as healthy and together as possible. No matter what shape you're in now, it's time to make fitness a chief concern.

It's not easy to get healthy in prison. It demands constant effort and self-discipline. So what are the advantages of busting your ass to stay healthy? You get:

1. **Strength of body:** greater resistance to illness, more able to defend yourself, and better prepared to cope with adversity.

2. **Stability of mind:** a cooler attitude, more self-confidence, and lower stress and hostility levels; improved sleep patterns; more on top of your game.

3. **Freedom to focus on spirit:** improved mental focus, more peace of mind, and greater ability to concentrate and meditate.

4. **Better preparation for release:** much better control of short setbacks; not as quick to go off on anybody.

5. **Increased success following release:** far better prepared to cope with the free world on all levels, especially finding a job and developing positive personal relationships.

In order to be truly fit, you have to increase your overall health in a variety of areas: physical, mental, emotional, social, educational, spiritual, vocational, and cultural. This is the true way to do battle with the system, as we discussed in "Beating the System." If you neglect any one of these areas, it will come back to haunt you because that is exactly where you'll be vulnerable! And the last thing you can afford in prison or in the community is an area of major weakness.

Stone Grocery Habit

"Garbage IN, garbage OUT!"

Unfortunately, the emotional stress of prison often drives people to do unhealthy things just when they most need their health. If a prisoner or family member is depressed, angry, or lonely, they can get in the habit of eating, smoking, or using some other addictive behavior as a way of coping with their feelings. This happens a lot on the streets and can sneak up on you while you're down. What appears to be an escape or relaxation is really making your problems worse, whether you face that fact or not.

It's easy to tell ourselves that our situation is pure misery and so we deserve what little relief we can get. We're just looking for some excuse to let ourselves **go**. This type of reasoning may have helped put us in prison. And our bodies and minds pay one hell of a price: short-term pleasure, long-term damage – not only to our health but to our self-respect and relationships with others.

We may get into chain smoking, coffee guzzling, or eating a lot of salty, greasy, sugary junk from the inmate store. This happens a lot to women prisoners when they miss their children or feel worthless or helpless. Some may have trouble dealing with the past – for instance if they have been sexually abused or thrown away by some dude they trusted. Or they may feel stupid for falling into the same traps over and over. So they just let themselves go – eat to forget. Then they put on a lot of weight and end up feeling even worse! They pay the real price after release because none of their clothes fit and, most of all, they feel fat and ugly.

These problems can and must be avoided! In fact, exercise is one of the best stress relievers you can find. Spend your time in prison getting healthy, and you will walk out of this trip much better off.

A 10 Milky Way Day

*"Morning and night I'd melt down 5 Milky Ways and drink 'em.
What a sugar rush! The problem was the crash;
it was like hitting a tank truck head on at 80!"*

One of the first great shocks for everyone who goes down is having to face the stuff they drop on your tray and ask you to believe it's food. If you didn't have to eat it to survive, you would think it was a cruel joke. Every place is different, some better than others, but none is the Holiday Inn. Overall, it is shameful the cold-blooded things they do to totally defenseless food.

Equally important is the type of foods served: fats, starches, and sugar, with very little protein and complex carbohydrates. The items that do have good nutritional value are often cooked so poorly that people refuse to eat them. We used our rock-hard pancakes as Frisbees until one wacked an assistant warden who stumbled into the line of fire. It crossed his eyes!

What happens, of course, is that many people try to live out of the inmate store. Too bad if their mothers have to up the monthly Social Security check, just as long as poor Bobby doesn't have to look that cold oatmeal in the eye. Supporting a hungry prisoner can be a real hardship for loved ones on a limited budget. And living off the junk from the store causes some very serious health problems as well.

Granted, the zoozoos and whamwhams seem a lot more appealing than prison slop. But take a look at what's in them; sugar, salt, fat, nicotine, caffeine, artificial flavors, preservatives, and a load of things you can't even pronounce! Not only is this stuff not good for you, many of these ingredients are stimulants that can make you edgy and out of control – a dangerous condition for a prisoner. The fact is, your diet has **a lot** to do with your ability to control your feelings and actions.

One of the keys to health, in and out of prison, is the right diet. Although your choices are seriously limited in prison, you must learn to "eat smart." You have to choose the most useful and avoid the most harmful. Review the earlier section "Physical Development" for some ideas on how to improve your diet while in prison.

Staying Healthy in a Cage

"If you get seriously sick in a joint, you may as well make out a will and kiss your mother goodbye."

The bad news is that **everyone** gets sick or hurt at some point while in prison. Some a little, some a lot. Many things come together to make prison a very unhealthy and dangerous place. Some dangers cannot be avoided. For instance, if one person in a cell block gets the flu from a visitor, everyone gets it. That's the main reason why so many leave prison with TB scars on their lungs.

Other dangers can sometimes be avoided. For example, some people get hurt while working on a tractor or in a metal shop, etc. Safety standards for prison labor are seldom carefully enforced. And everyone knows that it's easy to get off into a wreck with another inmate or the Man and end up needing a nose job. Since prison health care is not always up to free-world standards, it's smart to **stay alert**. Watch out for accidents or injuries which might require serious care or long-term treatment.

The good news is that many health problems can be avoided by simply taking care of yourself and using common sense. If you just follow the basic guidelines about food and exercise covered in the section "Physical Development" (pages 27-29), you can stay reasonably healthy. The healthier your body and mind, the better your ability to avoid problems, fight off illness, and recover as quickly as possible. Always look for ways to stay warm and dry, get enough rest, eat right, exercise, etc. **Learn to take care of yourself.**

This doesn't mean that people who work on their health don't have problems, too. But they don't have as many or as often, nor as intense and long-lasting. Those who take care of themselves are **much more together**, far more alert, stronger, quicker, and a lot more confident.

By taking care, I don't mean being able to fight or simply giving your body what it wants when it wants it. I mean giving yourself the care and the respect required to keep you fit, alert, and best able to respond to the world around you. That often means saying "no" to what tastes or feels good because you respect your own well-being. As an example, you have the good sense not to drink anti-freeze. Why? Because although it is very sweet to the taste, it is poison. So, too, are many types of food, drink, and other substances that might give us immediate pleasure.

Some people walk into prison with health problems, such as diabetes, hepatitis C, bad teeth, psychiatric problems, or a heart condition. This puts them in a bind, because if they demand help too loudly, they're labeled a "problem" and get shut down in one way or another. But if they are too humble and just go along for the ride, they won't get what they need.

When dealing with the medical personnel, be persistent but polite. Be patient but don't roll over and play dead; if you do, you are subject to end up that way. Try to be very "political"; ask a lot of questions from people who know what's happening and who's running things. Often inmate clerks control waiting lists, so a few store items can work wonders. But beware of people who claim to be able to "fix things" and fail to come across. Like everything else, you have to learn who you can count on; so don't ever pay for **anything** in advance.

Just as important as physical health is the need to stay mentally strong. This is hard work in a joint, but a healthy, balanced mind is the foundation for everything you do. For many people depression is a constant enemy that eats away at their sense of hope. Depression is like a black hole which will absorb all of your energy if you let it. To combat it, you must never believe its lies that life is hopeless and meaningless. Keep pursuing your spiritual growth to find the strength and stability essential to survival. **Constantly** search for the fresh energy and insight you need to support your growth.

A Special Word about AIDS

AIDS (acquired immune deficiency syndrome) is a major disease world-wide and has exploded in prisons across this country. There have been plenty of publicity and educational efforts to tell people how AIDS is spread and how to protect themselves. It is no longer an immediate death sentence, but infection with the AIDS virus has no cure or preventive vaccine. A person may go for years after infection with no symptoms, which is a major reason it has spread so rapidly. But once symptoms appear, survival depends on slowing the disease with intensive, ongoing treatment using expensive drugs.

This is a disease that people most often bring on themselves by having unprotected sex or sharing dirty needles. Outlaws are doing **far** more damage to themselves than the Man could ever hope to lay on them. Snap to the fact that it is not a man's disease, homosexual's disease, or white folks', black folks', or purple folks' disease. It kills **everyone** with total indifference!

So if you want to live, **protect yourself**. If the situation arises, use a condom during sex and avoid dirty needles, including tattoo equipment. You can find sources of more information on staying healthy and avoiding AIDS through your prison health services and library.

If you know you have been exposed to the AIDS virus or think you could be at risk, get tested. Nobody wants to get that kind of bad news, but you'll feel better longer if you get some help now – both medical and emotional – to deal with the disease. And for God's sake, don't spread it! Certainly your loved one has enough load to carry without that. And there is no glory in infecting a list of ignorant, careless fools who haven't got the sense to protect themselves.

Doing Battle With Anger and Hate

Anybody Seen My Armor?

"Like a turtle pulling into his shell for safety,
a prisoner withdraws by trying to be less
human, caring, feeling, and attached."

From the day you pulled the chain, you've been gradually adapting to the loss of identity and respect, to the chaos and lurking danger, because you have to. In so doing, you've changed in a lot of subtle ways. Mostly you will go to any extreme not to be vulnerable to anyone or anything, at any time or under any circumstance! When you first rolled up, you may have stuck your neck out a few times because you weren't hip to what was happening, only to have someone try to bash your brains out. Logically, since you don't get off on self-abuse, you quit.

By now you've learned that the prison trip consumes everything, so you must be on guard at all times. Day and night, seven days a week. To protect yourself you have slowly closed up on mental, spiritual, and physical levels. Now look within: have you become trapped in the very suit of armor you built to protect yourself?

If you notice you are losing the will or ability to make contact with people and things **outside of yourself**, your efforts for safety have become a trap. When you draw so far back that you become isolated from **yourself**, you face the greatest danger of all, the loss of hope. If this occurs, the prisoner and family feel that nothing else exists but the distress of the moment. Remember, if hope dies, **everything** dies. Hope is a basic need. You must **never** give it up, no matter what!

I Hate Your Mama!

"The rage in my heart is like an atomic reactor that's gone into meltdown! God help the poor bastards who catch the fallout."

Within the walls of concrete and steel, anger, pain, fear, and loneliness are the main courses on the menu. And, as you know, violence is often the dessert of choice. In addition, we are forced to accept often absurd rules and cope with insane pressures. When combined, these factors result in a dangerous charge of explosive **anger**.

This anger can spread until we include everything and everyone in our blind **rage**. We often use this rage in the way unlimited fuel dragsters use nitro: to propel us faster than the competition. Indeed, this may work for a few years, but it is extremely dangerous to us and to those around us. If we unleash it against the Man, other inmates, or ourselves, we face serious results. If we're not real careful, we can end up with fresh time or a tag on our big toe. And if we display it against our loved ones, as often happens in letters and visits, our most valued support can quickly vanish.

So we try to keep it all stuffed inside and handle the stress by doing more and more violence inside our heads. We may rehearse acts of vengeance and pretend to actually perform them as a way to release the pressure. But as the rage continues to grow, it begins to force its way to the surface. It turns into hate and finally becomes our deep-seated **passion**. At this point, we may not be able to control ourselves any longer. We **must** find workable ways to deal with all this poison inside ourselves!

I can tell you from my personal experience that giving in to hate is like drinking battery acid. I know now that I carried guns in the streets not for protection but because I was looking for someone to give me an excuse to shoot them. And, sure enough, I found one. So for me, prison only amplified negative things which were already there, probably since childhood. Being in the joint simply made me **more** bitter and dangerous.

But no matter where or when these feelings arise, each of us **can** and **must** learn to overcome our hostility. If we don't, we will be gradually swept away. Of the many dangers facing a prisoner, **none** is more serious and far-reaching. Staying in control of this is tough, but I give you my word that its importance cannot be overstated.

A Walking Time Bomb

"I could hear the bomb ticking inside my head. It kept getting louder and louder until I wanted to scream!"

Living behind a tidal wave of anger is a way of trying to protect ourselves from pain and fear. It is as though anger and violence become a drug we use to release stress or cover up our pain for a short time. We can gradually buy in to the false idea that whoever is close to us must be the cause of our pain and that our needs can be met by going off on people. In the end, we convince ourselves that the ideal way to solve our problems is to "go nuclear."

In this frame of mind, you can give yourself "permission" to actually do the mad-dog, radical things you used to only think about. It may happen in the joint or after release, when you least expect it. Again, this is a **very serious danger**. Not only do you run the risk of killing or being killed, you become a prime target for the prison staff, other inmates, state police, etc. All this does is take a bad situation and make it worse.

Take a good look in the mirror. Look back behind your eyes: do you see an explosive charge, **always** looking for something to set you off? If so, you need to learn to control it now. Otherwise, after three or four years in the pen you will blindly hate **everything and everybody**. This includes the system, those around you, and, too often, yourself and those who love you.

When you're overflowing with rage, you talk war and often take out your stress on those around you, even when you don't mean to. If this happens you have sentenced **yourself** to permanent exile, crushing any hope of rewarding bonds with family, friends, employers, and folks you've yet to meet. This is just another trap to steal a deeper part of your mind and soul!

So, if you find yourself wishing you were a trained assassin who could snuff everybody, **you have a problem!** This is a danger sign that cannot be ignored. Find the courage and help to overcome your demons, or they will eat you from the inside out. To do this, you **must** learn to control and direct your mind so that no one and nothing can make you dance like a puppet on a string.

Whenever you feel your anger about to erupt, it is **essential** that you confront and deal with it. You must recognize and work through your feelings. **Be very careful:** teach yourself to call a time-out before you go off on somebody. **Watch** how you are dealing with what's happening both inside and outside of you. Observe the way your mind is working. Step back, settle down, and see it all happening! **Listen** to how your mind talks to itself, to its tone and message.

Stay alert! Are you reacting to **real problems** or something of your own making? Is your reaction going to make things better or worse? What do you really want to get out of this situation? What choices do you have? Your ability to control how your mind and emotions respond is the **one true freedom** you have! While you cannot control the daily events of your life, you **can** and **must** control the ways you think and act! Don't react out of blind instinct; think about what's happening and respond in a way that is appropriate and useful. Review the earlier section "Reshape Your Thinking," for more ideas on ways to take control of your thoughts and actions.

Catch a Grip!

"These people think I'm bad?? Hell, I'll show them what 'bad' really means!"

At first it made you sick to watch the truly insane stuff that goes down in prison, but after a while you got numbed out in order to cope. As you watched the vile corruption around you, you began to develop a burning bitterness toward the system and the world that created it. For many inmates this means taking on a hostile attitude, an outlaw mentality, to help them survive and handle the pain. After years of bitterness and isolation, people sometimes take a strange pride in being an outcast, a "stone outlaw." For those who have been stripped of power and self-esteem, this can be a way to find an identity for themselves, even if a negative one.

Plus, prisoners sit around and tell endless lies and war stories about their gangster days and plans for future capers. Most of this is just a way to kill time, but it also feeds the feeling of "me against the square world." As time passes it's not surprising if you become consumed with the role of a professional outlaw. It provides a strong motivator, a fire that keeps your spirit alive! But be aware of the ultimate price: you can become a slave to something even more demanding than the Man. The further you fall off into this pit, the further you have to climb out again! There is nothing to be gained by becoming an "Ex-con from Hell." I learned this lesson the hard way.

Just because you watch others lose their grip doesn't mean **you** have to! Taking on a "ballistic" attitude and telling yourself you're a dangerous character may keep your motor running when you feel like you're out of gas. But it quickly becomes a personal demon. Don't buy in to the scam that you have to be a raging bad ass in order to keep your pride and dignity alive. This attitude is totally self-destructive; people who believe it will be a prisoner of themselves **long** after their bodies are released. You **must not** let this happen! Being a captive of the State is bad enough; becoming a captive of self-provoked madness is totally uncool.

Your biggest problems will come **after** release as you strive to shed the prison mentality and build a useful life. Prison games don't work in the community because the **rules** are different! Although both worlds can be heavy and strange, each calls for different ways of viewing life and responding to it.

Keep in mind that the more you play the prison game, the more garbage you have to carry out with you. The **only** thing prison values will do for you in the free world is put you right back in the pen. Doing time and hitting the bricks are hard enough; don't make them impossible by setting yourself up to fail!

It will be easier to handle your feelings if you keep physically healthy and fit. Review the sections "Physical Development" and "Health Needs in the Jungle" (pages 27-29 and 58) for suggestions on how to keep your body in shape. Healthy foods and exercise can make it easier to keep your emotions under control. And if you can find a friend, minister, or professional counselor to talk to, it will help you let off steam and get a different viewpoint on what is happening and other ways you can respond.

But the only long-term way to overcome hate and anger is through growth. It's only when you are focused on your own self-improvement that the garbage around you loses its importance. And it's only when you can look at yourself with pride and see how far you've come that you can forget about what others have done and what you'd like to do to them. There's only one real answer: outgrow the anger. Replace it with pride and peace of mind! So go back, review "Beating the System," and start putting it into practice. **Do it now!** If you let anger take over your life, then the system has won and you are a permanent part of the maze.

In the joint or in the streets, you must keep your mind and heart strong, honest, and focused in order to adjust to change without being eaten alive! Life in prison is, after all, just a lesson in how to come to grips with adversity. This challenge is always with us, no matter where we are.

Believe it or not, this issue is equally important for family members and friends of prisoners. Unless they find positive, healthy ways to balance their pain, loneliness, and fear, their lives get swallowed up in depression and anger. Study "Advice for Families of Offenders" (pages 102-124) for ways to understand and deal with all this.

Coping with Hard Time

Everything's Bad – That's Good!

"Some stand up and grow strong, some wither and die.
It's the same game but different players play it different ways."

So here you are, locked down like a rabid dog, being treated like you're ugly and stupid. No one in their right mind would seek such a plight. What you face as a convict is one of the most painful challenges anyone can experience.

But your situation has some hidden benefits that you may not recognize. Suffering is an essential part of everyone's life. From birth to death, we endure an inescapable series of painful events. As crazy as it may seem, pain can point the way toward growth. The more we suffer, the deeper we can look into our spiritual nature. And the more our spiritual nature deepens, the better we can understand reality and the secrets of life.

Thus, the pain we endure as prisoners can force us to grow further than we ever would have in the free world. But this will only happen if we stand up, face our suffering, and do battle with it! Many of us try to escape the pains of life by taking shelter in drugs, gambling, sexual extremes, or getting lost in another person. This won't solve our problems, but it **will** distract us from any possibility of learning from our suffering!

We also cannot gain from our labors if we **surrender** to the madness or sorrow of the moment. The loss of hope, just giving up, is an age-old trap! We need faith and determination to break out of blind despair. With every step forward, we gain a greater store of personal strength and insight. So, in a strange way, facing our suffering brings us rewards that cannot be gained any other way. This is why suicide (of mind, body, or spirit) is such a waste: when we give up, we lose the chance to use our stress and pain in order to grow.

Now is the time to commit yourself to **use** the pressure and hardship of the moment to temper your will, strengthen your mind, discipline your body, improve your judgment, and prepare for the future, be it a week away or 20 years. Use your suffering to awaken you to greater depths of feeling and insight. If you have to go through this garbage, why not get as much out of it as possible?

Nice idea, but it's a hell of a lot easier said than done! First, think of your situation as **survival training**. There isn't any school in the world that will teach you what you can learn about yourself and others inside a joint! This is not to say you want to be there, but while you are, why not use it to the max? Watch how you think and act; examine your values and behavior on every level.

Don't just lie on your bunk and listen to your heartbeat. Have the honesty and courage to face what you find inside yourself. Anything you don't like or that doesn't work **can be changed!** While folks are running around in the streets eaten up with nickel-and-dime garbage, you have a rare chance to search for the roots of who you are and what you want your life to be. Make prison work for you. Take your punishment and turn it into triumph!

Say, Did My Watch Stop?

"My cell partner said time had stopped.
I looked at my watch and told him he was crazy…
it was actually running backwards!"

Doing time, in prison or on the streets, works in cycles. There are high and low points. At the low times everything seems to **stop**. This usually happens after a crisis, such as when an appeal or parole falls through. A family crisis, such as an unexpected divorce or the death of a loved one, can also make the clock seem to quit ticking.

These are dangerous periods; hope gets thin and both inmates and loved ones think, "Why bother?" Be careful when things go into a depressed state. It's easy to slide into a "don't give a damn" attitude. If you become consumed with sad and desperate feelings, it usually leads to crazy or violent behavior, and this only compounds the problems. But don't lose faith: as long as the sun keeps coming up and going down, time **is** passing.

The secret to dealing with these slow times is to **keep busy!** Beware of stress, depression, and self-pity. Don't just sit around and pick your nose; and becoming a TV junkie won't fix things, either. Find ways to challenge your mind and develop your body. This is not a time to just glide along! Get involved in something positive, and everything will work out. Remember: while you have many physical limits, what you can do inside your head is **boundless!**

For Long-Termers and Lifers

For People Doing Five to Ten

One of the worst things about doing major time is living around people who aren't! The shorter the sentence, the more people snivel, bitch, and moan. Too often they refuse to let you do your time in peace, steadily stirring up some kind of storm that threatens your routine. This is an issue you will learn to endure as you adjust and build yourself a niche.

For you, the greatest problem is not physical danger as much as mental stagnation. If prison food doesn't kill you, boredom just might! Survival depends on your will and ability to keep life "moving." This is very difficult because you cannot afford to get lost in events in the world. **But** being totally consumed by prison life is an equal trap, so what do you do?

You develop creative ways to **become strong of mind and body!** People doing short beefs can get by just letting their fingernails grow…but for you, doing time is not a joke or a picnic. Each day you are faced with a crossroads: one way goes up, the other down. There are no other options. Having the courage and will to face adversity is far more beneficial for you than simply surviving this demanding situation.

You'll eventually exit prison with the ability to see deep into people and situations far better than those who have never been to prison ever will. Beyond mere "information," you will possess a deep understanding of human nature, good and bad. But for now your challenge is to sustain hope at all costs while being honest with yourself as to what is required for you to achieve your dreams and ambitions.

For Those Doing Ten to Forever

You are part of a special group of people who pay the highest price, the full-time residents of hell, including lifers who strive every day to make a home in one of the least hospitable places on Earth. It's your world. Others just "visit" but you live here. As such, you are people I am deeply concerned about while having little useful insight to offer you.

If you have recently arrived with six car loads of time, no doubt you are in deep shock and disbelief. One old friend, upon return from court in 1969 with a fresh double life sentence, described the sensation as falling off the edge of the world. Fifteen years later he said his ability to sustain hope required "finding ways to be useful." It was by defining a series of positive purposes that he both survived and expanded his mind and will.

This is not a simple task, in or out of prison. But I've grown to believe it can be done no matter where you are, so long as you have the determination and courage to do so.

I cannot express too often the fact you will experience a wide range of difficult ups and downs. But even in here change never stops! This means no matter what dark cloud comes over you, it will not stay more than six weeks…as long as you just **let it go!**

I have never personally been faced with ten to forever, so I cannot speak from firsthand experience. But I have known many who have, and it requires a very settled, balanced mind. The secret is discipline of your emotions! This includes a daily routine that allows you private time to read, think, and mentally exist far beyond the tiny confines of a prison.

Last, there is a great advantage to practicing basic breath meditation. Why? Because what "meditation" really means is "connecting with the universe." Consider how important it is for a prisoner to be able to tap into such a storehouse of power! And it is available to you 24/7 – an ability no one can take from you as long as you live!

Ultimately, no matter how much time you're doing or the conditions you are called upon to endure, every day is an opportunity to remain vital and engaged with life. You have the opportunity to develop an inner strength few if any citizens will ever come to know. As a result, you will amass a rewarding sense of personal pride and self-worth.

"For most people prison is just a chapter in their lives…
for some it's the whole damned book!"

For the past 30 years, state and federal legislatures have passed laws putting greater numbers of people away for longer periods. All it takes is for one mad dog ex-con to do something really gross for citizens to become outraged and scream for the blood of "all those criminals."

So politicians sponsor new laws to show they are champions in the latest "war against crime." As a result, they pass harsher sentencing guidelines and habitual criminal statutes, elimination of good time and parole, and tons of other items off the D.A.'s wish list as a way to "flush" you rather than "punish" you.

So how does the advice in this book serve those who are **trapped** in the maze? What use is it to men and women who have been "thrown away" and have no choice but to adjust and cope? I'm not talking here about the "turn arounds" who get out before they know how to find the chow hall. I mean those of you who are being ground up and fed to the hogs!

A Map Through the Maze is about a very special journey…one no one would ever choose. For lifers and people doing **serious** time, many things in this book may appear useless. They may not seem to relate to someone doing more time than King Kong could carry. But such a view is inaccurate.

Personal Growth

"A Mississippi lifer said my work was like 'teaching self-help to zombies.'" "I told him even the living dead can dream of a better day. He laughed!"

All this rah-rah jive about personal growth – does it **really** make any sense for a five-time loser looking at 2033 for relief? It may not seem to on the surface. You have to stop and **really** look at it. One can say, *"I'm a lifer, so why bother to care or try or even hope?"* But that is an emotional reaction based on a moment of depression, a sad point of view. The truth is: **life is not over till the light goes out!** So the more time you have to carry, the **more** you need strength of mind and heart, and the **more** the ideas in this book apply to **you**. Frankly, the need for personal discipline and development is 100 times greater for someone doing 10 years than a person doing 10 months!

We were not born to "party hardy" but to come to an ever-growing understanding of ourselves. Every moment we live is a new and unique chance to find greater inner power and peace. No matter how harsh, **anything** that forces us to look life in the eye gives us a chance to grow! In truth, we can often achieve a higher purpose in life just as effectively in prison as anywhere else.

It is of little comfort to a prisoner doing serious time, but in truth you are very different from 99% of mankind. While the public is caught up in the countless distractions of daily life, you don't have to wade through the silly trash that eats people up in the streets. Even though you didn't choose it, your situation frees you to go within yourself and explore remote corners of your mind and spirit.

This chance to get away from the idiocy of the general public is what monks and wise men have sought for centuries. For a person who has so much time they cannot see light at the end of the tunnel, you can achieve your freedom by looking within yourself and letting go of old cravings and attachments.

Granted, a joint is not a monastery filled with peaceful vibes! But after five years or more, existence in prison just becomes the same old routine. So you can shift your attention and use the time as a unique chance to **focus within!** Use it, treasure it, take advantage of this chance to find truth within the center of your being. There is a world within you just as great and powerful as the world outside of you. Find it, explore it, learn to live in that deeper reality! It's the key that can give you freedom.

Never Surrender Your Mind!

"There are only two things prisoners truly own: the power of their will and the quality of their mind."

By now you've been down more than a few Christmas Eves – so you are no stranger to the insanity of a cell block! You know that, when a person is being held by force and threatened with severe punishment, it is often necessary for them to comply with the defined rules of daily life. But being a captive does not mean you should abandon yourself! It is not necessary for you to sink into the quicksand of dishonesty, hatred, isolation, bitterness, and **hopelessness** that spread in prison like a cancer. As I have said before, prison may have your body, but it cannot command your will or your mind – unless **you** surrender them. No matter who does what to mess with you, you must **never, ever** surrender control of your dignity, hope, or mental processes. It doesn't matter if you are doing 20 months or 20 flat years, the principle is the same.

If your body is attacked and you don't die, it *can* heal. If you get lost in depression but refuse to give up, you can recover. And when someone jacks with your understanding, you **can** fight their influence and get your balance back. Your ability to think and reason is your tie to reality, and it's 100% **yours**. It gives you the capacity to grow and the will to hold on against all obstacles. Cherish and protect it at all costs!

The best way to hold on while living in captivity is to build a safe haven within yourself. **Not** just a brief escape from your pain but a positive, constructive way to weather **all** the storms that threaten to overwhelm you. Even though the world around you is sick and shallow, that doesn't mean you must be the same. Fight back by finding and following your own sense of values. **Personal growth** is the only life raft you have when you get this far out to sea! Although your progress may seem slow, your willpower and self-respect grow stronger every time you refuse to let the energy of the joint "take" you.

Reflect, meditate, go within to develop your spiritual nature. Read, study, help others, learn to draw, write science fiction, play baseball, make belts, feed the birds in the yard, write poetry, stay in touch with world events, work out, play music. Do **anything** positive or healthy to keep from getting lost in prison dishonor, self-pity, and anger against yourself and/or the world. Although things around you are ugly and stupid, you can find beauty and a reason for hope within your own heart and will. But it will not just come to you. As when searching for a precious diamond, you must dig deep to find it.

Looking for the Door

The Carrots: Appeals, Pardons, and Paroles

"Nose first or toes first, everyone gets out!"

Clearly the first two rules concerning prison life are to **survive** and to **get out!** And most inmates do, in fact, live through it and finally exit. There are different ways people try to obtain release. The "creative" ways are hitting the fence, digging a tunnel, dressing up like a nun, etc. The traditional – and more permanent – ways are appeals, pardons, and paroles. Most people end up being released on parole or discharging their sentence.

As we discussed earlier in the section "I'm Gonna Appeal," an inmate and his/her family often hold themselves together after sentencing by hoping for a successful appeal. After a few years of intense effort and concern, that doesn't work so they may decide to push for a pardon. A pardon, in most cases, is just grasping at straws; the odds against it are so great **no inmate should expect it to be successful.**

Successful pardons or time cuts (also called a commutation of sentence) are as rare as hen's teeth. In some cases, they are based on the merits of the case or the reversal of an unjust sentence. But more often, the very few pardons granted are political favors, and most inmates and families just don't have the juice (power and money) to make that happen. You **may** have a shot if the real villain finally confesses or new DNA evidence appears, the D.A. requests a commutation, and the media backs it. And you know how rare such things are.

My experience suggests that most people try for appeals and/or pardons for two reasons. Their sentence is so heavy they cannot see daylight and this is the way they choose to keep from giving up. Or they are looking for a way to occupy themselves as they build enough time to become eligible for parole.

If you want to go after an appeal or a pardon, the best general rule is to **do your homework first**. Serious homework! Don't put your fate in the hands of a jailhouse lawyer if you can help it. Although some are very competent, you are often wasting your hope and groceries.

You should certainly learn all you can from inmates who have insight and experience. But appellate law is THE most complex aspect of criminal law and requires some very special skills which few prisoners have. Study the laws and get all the help you can inside. Then, if you think you have a shot and are within the time limits, try to get your case (and transcripts) before an appeals attorney on the streets.

Warning: do not invest your life savings in an appeal, pardon, or parole effort! It's not necessary and in most cases will not do any good. Also, beware lawyers or private consultants who take advantage of an inmate's or family's desperation by giving them false hopes. If you hire an attorney, have a well-defined contract *and* a clear idea of how long it will take. Many such efforts take **years** and the prisoner is already free by the time the case comes up for review!

So for most people, release comes by parole or discharge on a defined date. If you have a probable release date, then, for better or worse, you **know** what you're looking at. But if you are dealing with a state parole process, it can be a big guessing game.

Parole can become the Great Crusade for both the inmate and loved ones. Often everyone looks forward to it and makes **a huge investment** of **time**, energy, money, and, most of all, hope. It can be a long, draining ordeal and drag you into a state of deep emotional distress. The danger comes when you place **all** your hopes and resources on any one effort for release. If the bottom falls out, you don't have anything else to stand on!

The Old Turn-Down Blues

"Hey, didn't you hear me? I said I was sorry!"

Keep in mind that the appeals, pardons, and parole processes are just as insane and hard to understand as the courts and the prison system. In addition, the institution often has control over your good time rates and awards, which really keeps you dancing. So don't be shocked if they jack you around, string you out, give you false hopes, and then cut your throat.

Try to be prepared for the mental and emotional letdown that comes with a turn-down, denial, or set off. There are no words to describe it but anyone who has lived it will fully understand. This event is equally hard on the family because they have often placed all their hopes for relief on the success of this effort. The natural reaction is disappointment and wanting to know why. Don't be surprised if you never get a straight answer. Punishment is far from an exact science.

Remember that the final goal is to get out and stay out, so save some mental and physical resources for the future. If you invest everything in each new effort, three or four denials or set-offs can throw a prisoner and his family into mental, emotional, and even financial bankruptcy. This is another blind turn in the maze and can lead to expanded bitterness and burn-out. So, no matter where you are in the process, don't let the system or your false hopes break you or your loved ones.

My advice to **both** inmates and families is this: no matter how crazy or heavy things get, don't crawl under a log and die. It's okay to pause and rest from time to time but you **must** do whatever it takes to keep yourself strong and united. The appeal, pardon, and parole processes are but single steps in this whole journey; don't let them eat you. Whatever happens, stay cool and don't go off on anybody. Hope for the best but be prepared for the worst. Some folks get out sooner, some later. Your time will come, so hang on. If you lose hope now, they have you forever!

Getting Short

99 Days and a Get Up

*"I held my breath the last three months
and pretended I was the Invisible Man!"*

It's odd how different people count their time. A person doing a dime counts years. A person doing a year counts months. A person doing months counts days. And a person doing days counts hours. Each has a different frame of mind but all have a common goal: freedom! So for each, release becomes the top priority, often excluding all other factors.

When an inmate finally begins to get short, he or she goes through a whole bunch of conflicting, frightening thoughts and feelings. For someone who has only been down 12 months in a work camp, it will be much more light-weight than for someone who has been buried for 12 years in Leavenworth. The more times the world has turned since an inmate fell off into prison, the more dizzy he or she will be the day they are kicked out.

When you get down to the last 100 days or so from exit everything gets real weird. Most inmates and families feel an intense mixture of hope and fear about what the future holds. You get nervous and edgy and it looks like the Man is trying to trap or goad you into making a bad move. And on top of every other problem, you have to cope with the hardest factor to control – **yourself**.

These "short pains" are **very** real and affect both the mind and body. This is a time of extreme anxiety when everyone tries to gear up and get ready. You may get the strong impression that those around you are out to get you. And, look here, they probably are! As you know, jealousy is a monster inside the small world of a prison. So be super careful to avoid any heat from any source. And, whatever you do, don't run around telling everyone, *"Man, I'm so short I could fit my whole body into a matchbox!"* Just keep your mouth shut!

As you struggle to prepare for release, inmates and their loved ones should each get a copy of *99 Days and A Get Up*. This book can help take the edge off a scary time and better prepare you for life after prison. Use this material to help prepare your survival plan and get your head ready for the reality shift. Also study *Man, I Need a Job!* to prepare for getting and keeping a job. Job hunting is a real challenge and you owe it to yourself to be as ready as possible. And, last, if you have any form of dependency or addiction problem, read *Life Without a Crutch* as an important step in staying free of dependency and enjoying life. All are on page 129.

The Moment of Truth

"On the surface you try to look mellow.
You don't want anybody to know that inside your
guts it's like Custer's last stand!"

Now, as you strive to get ready to hit the bricks, you feel as though you are about to play a game of world-class poker with a pair of deuces! All the anxiety you went through when you first went down comes roaring back. With it come sleepless nights, loss of appetite, and six tons of stress and dread.

As you get **really short**, fear of the unknown begins to nibble at your brain like a hungry rat. The same concerns affect your family and loved ones. They get really worried that suddenly Mr. Bad Ass or Ms. Trouble is actually coming home. What will happen? More of the same? Were the promises real? This is a moment of truth. If you have spent years feeding yourself and the world a lot of jive or living off false hopes, **Now** is the time to get your heart and head right.

Your mind plays a lot of tricks on you the closer you get to the door. You just know in your heart something horrible is going to happen to prevent your actual exit. A new detainer? A screw up in the paper work? A setup and five years new time? It gets **real crazy!**

The last week is sheer agony. No sleep, not much food...just holding your breath. Trying hard not to give off any "I'm short" vibes. Staying away from old enemies; dodging the hacks who hate you. Wanting to give your stuff away to the few you care about but being too paranoid to do it.

Now is a good time to do a mental and emotional inventory, sorting out the positive lessons you've learned from the junk you've collected. Make every effort to recognize and eliminate the mental and emotional garbage that have built up in prison. As we've seen, such feelings often become a way of life. If so, you may not even realize how angry or hostile you have become. But unless you're St. Peter, you probably have many negative emotions going on deep inside.

A week before I left the joint the second time, I wrote a list of the things that had most hurt and angered me. In my mind I thought it would only take 30 minutes and one page of paper. In fact it took three days and nights and a full notebook! It was shocking to uncover the mountain of bad feelings I had against so many things and people, especially myself (not to mention the snitch). Then, the night before I left, I put the notebook in a trash can, lit the sucker up, and laughed a lot!

It is so important to do everything you can to leave your anger and "attitude" behind. In your mind, declare your roles as "slave" and as "criminal" to be over: **let them go!** Do not walk out the gate with this old baggage.

It is vital to relax, do a lot of deep breathing, and practice extra patience on all fronts. Surely the last thing you want to do is get sideways with **anyone**. The safest approach is to get real quiet, stick to yourself, and begin to cut yourself loose from the way things are done in the pen. (But be careful not to let your mind leave while your body is still inside.)

This is also the time to look at the very powerful issue of **fear**. It does no good to pretend it doesn't exist. The longer you've been down, the greater your discomfort will be over the uncertain future. You will naturally feel stress about your upcoming role in the free world. But the work you've done inside yourself while a captive and the quality of your plans will help keep the stress under control. Chill out, focus on self-control, and don't sweat the small stuff.

It's not unusual to feel guilty or sad for being able to leave while people you care about are still stuck shuffling up and down the halls. But you didn't carry them in with you and you don't get to carry them out. Everyone has their yoke to pull; their turn will come, too. Just give them all your gear, wish 'em well, and move on.

6

Rebirth and Beyond:
Release to Success

The Rush of Release

Kicked Out of the Joint!

*"When they came to cut me loose I told 'em I had some
unfinished business, to come back in an hour.
The Major said leave NOW or be drug out feet first.
They never were big on hospitality!"*

THE DAY THEY cut you loose begins like any other: the sun comes up, the shifts change, and the joint slips into its dull old routine. One would think that after all your excitement and expectation there should be a parade with marching bands and a cheering crowd. But, no, they just tell you to pack your shit, sign some papers, and get the hell off government property. Ready or not, **you get kicked out!**

As you ride away and look back, all you see are faceless people doing what you did yesterday...and countless mornings before that. The only real difference is that tonight someone else will be in your bunk – because you're damn well gone!

Suddenly you perceive that this place, which has been the center of your life for so long, is nothing more than a tiny fly speck on the side of a narrow little back road, outside a quiet little town. The only thing that ever gave it any importance was your presence. Then you turn away and face forward – into the future with all its challenges, options, risks, and rewards.

Your space ship has now returned from Penal Colony X to Planet Earth and beamed you down to a noisy, nasty Greyhound bus station. The return is as shocking as the day you pulled the chain! Remember what you went through adjusting to the joint? Now you begin to go through the same thing, except **backwards**, as you start the long process of adjusting to the streets. The deeper they had you buried and the longer you've been away, the harder it will be, because so much has changed. Indeed, **everything** has changed – especially you.

Wow, I'm OUT – or am I?

"So tell me the truth, is my brand showing?"

The day you hit the bricks, you will not feel "free." In fact, aside from your desire to get the hell down the road, you may not feel much of anything, because you will be numb. This is perfectly natural. Your body and mind are working overtime to absorb all the changes that come with suddenly being thrown into the intense demands and speed of modern life. If you're like most folks, you just go into a mild state of shock. It would be no different if suddenly you returned from five years on an island in the South Pacific. Your body is out here, but the rest of you is still back there.

Don't let this worry you. There is nothing you can do to change or hurry things up. Just understand what's going on and try to relax and go with the flow. Keep telling yourself to calm down and accept the fresh wonder of it all. Try to suspend your mind and simply experience the explosion of new sights and sounds. The first week or two are sort of a blur. In fact, many newly released people say they feel as though they are on a furlough and not really free.

As the initial shock begins to wear off, the first thing you feel is different from everyone else. It is as if squares can look at you and see "CRIMINAL" branded across your forehead. This is a strong feeling that cannot just be ignored, but it's absolute rubbish. The only time your past really shows is if you play gangster, let your anger hang out, or run the dull old game of "scare the squares."

The second thing you experience is depression! This is very confusing because you expect someone just out of prison to be on top of the world. But the extreme nature of the changes you must make is very unsettling and draining. Relax; you are not going crazy. Such feelings are a natural part of the radical shift in reality an ex-con faces. They may come and go during the first year or so before you have your balance. In most cases, they will simply pass with time. However, if you find yourself being overwhelmed by depression, or any emotion, **go get help!**

One thing for sure: release from captivity is an exciting and wonderful event. To suddenly move from a state of no choice into one of abundant options can be the rush of a lifetime. Like blasting full speed down the steep bank of a roller-coaster, it's a sensational **thrill!** Savor the moment!

Be Cool, Fool

*"A former prisoner can be a living hand grenade,
just walking around looking mellow until some
small thing pulls his or her pin."*

While in prison, many people lose touch with their true feelings and can't recognize what's actually buried inside. When this happens, they may feel calm and in control for a few weeks or months after release, only to go into fits of irrational behavior, anger, or depression later on. This is often brought to the surface by anxiety from two classic traps: **wanting too much too soon and expecting the impossible.**

The anxiety doesn't really hit you at first because you're busy just looking around and enjoying the show. But as you accept your freedom and try to start functioning, the stress of so many changes can bring up old feelings. If you don't deal with these buried feelings, they may explode. You will find yourself reacting to a new situation based on old prison ways of thinking and acting. You'll be shocked to hear what comes out of your mouth – as if it were another person speaking! Although this is a natural result of having been in prison, it can seriously endanger your welfare and ties throughout the community.

Prison may not be to blame for all of these feelings. For many folks, their hostile attitude helped put them in the joint to begin with. That attitude may have come from past abuse – physical and emotional scars they received as a child. As adults, they may not understand where those scars came from or what to do about them. And prisons have a 225-year history of making the damage much worse!

But no matter how much abuse we've suffered (both in and out of prison), it doesn't justify passing that pain on to others. Too often we act out against the very people who stood by us, or total strangers who just happen to be on hand. Beware of this trap! It can crush your hope for the future and kill any chance of getting along with others, not to mention getting you locked up again.

On top of everything else, you will **know** that what you're doing is not right for your new situation. But you don't have the skills yet for a more practical response. When you are fresh out, you still have a foot in both worlds. This leads to a lot of confusion and mental torment, so slow down and give yourself some slack. **Cool your jets!**

If you find yourself doing any of the above, take it seriously. Don't just try to look the other way! Many ex-cons ignore disruptive thoughts or actions until things get out of control and they are in a major crisis. They may try to cope by getting stoned just to "take the edge off," but this does nothing to resolve their problems. A few hours later the problems are still right there, even worse than before!

So keep an eye on your pressure gauge. When you see the needle approaching the red zone, go find a friend, minister, or counselor to help you cope with this difficult time. Many people don't bother to seek help because life in the joint convinced them they are totally alone and cut off from the world. Often prisoners get into the ego trip of thinking that a **real** man or woman shouldn't need help from others or that no one could possibly understand them. But this attitude is false. In truth, there **are** capable people who understand what you are going through and can help you develop the skills to work through your feelings. So don't hesitate to seek and accept any type of help that will improve the quality of your life.

Now What?

"Sleeping in a piano crate, standing in a soup line, and living like a bum is NOT my idea of freedom!"

Every person who exits a jail or prison must deal with basic survival needs. In order to meet these needs, a realistic plan is essential. Planning for the future is discussed in more depth in *99 Days and A Get Up* and *Man, I Need a Job!* (see page 129). Most prisoners try to construct a plan while down, but after release they quickly find that it was based more on wishful thinking than functional reality. When this happens, they must be ready to revise their plans, daily if necessary.

When we are in a survival mode, we tend to let everything slide except our immediate needs. We think about only what is in front of us. This is normal and unavoidable. It was also our primary way of life in prison. But in order to build a balanced life, we need to work from a balanced plan that takes all of our needs into consideration. As we make progress, we can shift some of our attention, energy, and resources from survival to other parts of our plan.

To be balanced, a basic survival plan should include:

1. A survival budget and source of needed funds
2. Employment
3. Family/personal support (including child care, if needed)
4. Housing
5. Transportation
6. Health care
7. Legal concerns and parole
8. Recreation
9. Personal growth: education and training
10. Spiritual nourishment and growth

Some of these areas focus on basic get-down survival, while others are part of our long-term development, as discussed in "Balance Your Growth" on pages 24-36) earlier in this book. Plans are best developed in two time frames: short-term (the first six to 12 months) and long-term (the next two to five years). As short-term needs are met, the emphasis will shift to long-term growth and self-improvement. To help reduce some of the confusion and anxiety, it is also smart to create a specific plan just for that first, crazy week on the outside.

There is limited support available in the community to help you meet some of your survival needs. But the help won't come looking for you. Nobody in the free world thinks they owe you a favor because you've done a taste of time. And the rumors about wonderful programs such as Supplemental Security Income (SSI) and Small Business Administration (SBA) loans just waiting for released prisoners are total garbage. Ninety-nine percent of your progress will depend on **you** to make realistic plans and then to find and use the opportunities you need. The book *Man, I Need a Job!* gives more information on finding help in the community.

A special word of caution: over the past 38 years I have watched countless ex-cons struggle with the difference between what they want and what they can get. Next to anger and isolation, no other single thing seems to create so much stress. There is an intense drive to get back up as quickly as possible, but it **never** happens fast enough or to the degree hoped for. Again, do not set yourself up to fail by expecting too much from yourself and the world.

It helps to think of yourself as **new to town**, which is true. And with any newcomer, certain dues are required. For someone moving from Dallas to Seattle, it may take two years to get settled and five years to get halfway comfortable. The best way to cope is to set small goals that can be achieved in the near future. Rather than plan to "get a good job paying $100,000," plan to "get up tomorrow at 7 a.m. and complete applications for the four employers you identified yesterday." Your progress for the first few years will be painfully slow. But keep yourself under tight control and you will watch your progress grow like a snowball rolling down a hill!

Man, I Need a Job!

> *"A job is important not only for survival but because it offers a valuable way to begin feeling better about yourself after prison."*

Shortly after release a former prisoner has to deal with the need for a job. A job is a basic part of survival and meeting the rules of parole. For ex-cons, this presents a series of special problems based on the economy, a criminal record, fear of failure, lack of current skills, the need for transportation, and many other factors.

Finding and keeping a job is hard even for well-prepared squares. It is far more difficult for people with a criminal past! So it makes sense to do as much preparation as you can toward success in the job market. A lot of what it takes to get and keep a job is **mental**. Although you may not actually score a gig from inside a cell, you be setting goals, learning new skills, and working on your attitude and self-control. Your mental attitude determines your self-confidence and the way you present yourself. Therefore, the better you come to terms with your own criminal history, the better you'll be able to look an employer in the eye and sell your value as a person.

Before and after release, you can help yourself prepare to find a job by reading *Man, I Need a Job!* This handbook discusses general job search skills as well as ways to deal with your criminal history. Continue to review it during your actual job search, while adjusting to the workplace, and later when you're ready to look for a better job. There are some unique attitudes and skills an ex-con really needs to prepare for a rewarding job. A lot of useful ideas will jump out at you just when you need them.

The First Taste of Freedom

A New World, a New You

"It's an all-new game. New rules, new players and the score is 0 to 0. Use what you learned in the joint but if you pistol-whip your mother, you're going to catch a penalty."

Getting out is one side of the coin; staying out is the other. Release from prison is not the solution to your problems! It's just the midpoint of a much larger, more complex experience. In a sense, it's as if you are being reborn. The ways of thinking and acting you picked up in prison are now **dead and stinking!** Along with all the anxiety and confusion of release, you have the chance to decide who you really want to be.

Inmates tend to carry tons of mental and emotional garbage out of prison with them. They often hit the streets consumed with hostile feelings and less in control of themselves than the day they went down. Plus, they tend to be withdrawn and unable to trust anyone. They may show mistrust and blind resentment toward everything and everybody they come into contact with. So it's normal for people just out to feel anxious and lost at times.

Many ex-cons try to handle their uncertainty with hostility and jailhouse jive. But this just keeps them isolated from those around them. If you want to be rejected and fail to get along with anyone, all you have to do is play Professional Ex-Con. I admit that I wore my mean mask for a long time because I thought it would protect me from the vultures. Perhaps it did in a few cases. But it mostly cut me off from any hope of loving or being loved. I mean, who wants to kiss a cobra? Only another cobra! And that's not the kind of company you want to keep.

Until you are able to become a part of the world after release, you're not yet free. The Man still has you! Although it only took one heartbeat for your body to leave the joint, your mind won't leave until it has something more positive to attach itself to out in the world. So kick back and be patient. As time passes you will focus more on street issues and less on prison war games. It just takes a little effort and a lot of patience, but you can do it!

In addition to hostility and mistrust, being locked up can also cause prisoners to lose their sense of **identity and purpose**. Thus it's normal for a person fresh out to wonder who they are and how to carry themselves. The basic rule in society is this:

you are what you do! As discussed in the earlier section "Seek the Right Path," if you act in positive ways which result in benefits for yourself and the world around you, you're a "good" person, worthy of respect and support. On the other hand, if you act in negative, selfish ways that benefit you at the expense of others, you're a "bad" person. If this is your choice, you can expect to be disliked, rejected, and possibly punished.

Life in the joint says you have to be nasty and cold-blooded to get over on others. The question is, do you want to be a slave to an idea that results in failure and rejection? Or are you ready to find a new way to relate to yourself and other people? One key to true freedom and satisfaction is having the respect of both yourself and others. To score this, you have to be right with people, giving them the respect, kindness, honesty, tenderness, and concern that you yourself hunger for.

As you re-establish contact with family and friends, try to lighten up. Remind yourself to relax and take it easy. With new people, be cautious and take your time, but also stay open to an exchange of energy and concern. This doesn't mean it's always safe to be a trusting, decent person. From time to time some shark will come along and try to pick your bones clean. Clearly there is risk attached to being an honest, caring human being. But if you use the hard-core insight you've learned in the joint and on the streets, you will be very careful who you let get next to you. Pick your target. It's smart business to be selective – but don't run and hide; be open to positive interaction with others!

Keep in mind that being a good person doesn't require being somebody's chump. It means basing your thoughts and actions on what you believe is decent and right. Stay alert. Don't be guided by what looks good, smells sweet, or tells you what you want to hear. That's probably what put you in the joint to begin with. I'm sure you understand.

Relighting the Flame

"The first year I was down, fun died. The second year, laughter;
the third, tenderness; the fourth, love. By the time
they finally cut me loose, there was nothing
left but echoes and an attitude."

Obviously one of the hardest and most important adjustments ex-cons have to make is in dealing with people. As you know, prison breeds mistrust of strangers. At the same time, it tends to distance you from your ability to be **intimate and loving**. You can "think it," write poems about it, dream of it, but you don't really know how to do it!

The walls you build to protect yourself from others can become your own prison. They end up keeping you in and everybody else out, even the ones you want to let in. In this way your heart becomes a lonely castle with a drawbridge you've forgotten how to let down. Your mind remembers how it used to be, but all the gears and chains are so rusty nothing works the way it should. This is a real problem when you come back to someone you love and with whom you want to be deeply personal.

On top of everything else, you're not sure if what you feel is real. Maybe you made it up in a half sleep one cold night with a pillow over your head – like all those love letters with a billion promises of things "we're going to do when I get home" – you know. But when you get honest, you know that much of what you put in those letters was serious, well-intended fairy tales. It was an image of what you want to be, not who you really are. It was a way of holding onto one another in a sick, unnatural state. Each of you tried to say what you thought the other wanted or needed to hear in order to keep your love alive.

But now **it's show time!** It's a hell of a shock to come home to your "soul mate" and snap to the fact you are total strangers. You have to learn all over again to touch, be tender, close, and intimate. If this is a 100% jailhouse romance and the only place you've touched was in a visiting yard, both of you had better fasten your seatbelts. It's going to be a rocky ride!

Like everything else, starting or re-starting an intimate relationship takes time, good intentions, patience, and humor. Frankly, if you jump right into bed, it is a critical error. First, you must build a bridge of tenderness and honesty in the real world that will support the weight of your years of heavy-duty promises and concern. Get to know one another. Keep things light and easy. Go out and play! But do yourself a big favor: stay away from drugs and booze. You already have enough problems trying to get your head and heart together. Alcohol or drugs will twist every thought and feeling and make a hard trip simply impossible. Doing it **right** is the right thing to do.

Let me say it again: **don't sweat the sex stuff**. You have waited for years, so a few weeks (or even months!) of "romancing" isn't going to kill you. In fact, honest sharing of your feelings and fears can be much more intimate than anything your body can do. And never fear, it's like riding a bicycle; you never totally forget how! Plus, if you do fall off, it's not very far to the ground. Just remember, you are fresh out of a joint and your partner is scared to death. There is no way on earth all those sex-crazed fantasies in all those letters are going to actually happen. And if they do, it will be much later on. So don't damage this important relationship by trying to do the impossible.

While you were down, you did one of two things: set the stage for the success of your relationship or set it up to fail. It all depends on how you approached it. If it was just a life raft, just a way to do your time, then you can do whatever you wish. It will end within a matter of weeks or months after you walk. If, on the other hand, your relationship has real meaning for you and you want it to work, certain things have to happen both before and after release.

In the earlier section on "Personal Ties," I stress the absolute need for a true friendship. This is the key that unlocks the drawbridge; it is the factor which turns mere illusion into something real, solid, and good. In order to be true friends, you must learn to get close to each other without getting lost and surrendering your identity. You must be separate individuals even while sharing your love. This is very hard for "love junkies" to relate to. Believe me, I know. I used to fall in love with total strangers on elevators between floors!

In order to develop a relationship that will give us closeness and room to be ourselves, we must learn how to **bond** without **abandoning** ourselves. Then we can let down our defensive walls and get close to another person without destroying our relationship or ourselves in the process. The ability to balance self with others is one of the true secrets to a quality life. Once we have learned to do it, we will also have a greater ability to build new, fresh relationships with the people we meet in daily life. And we will make wiser choices about when to let down our guard and who we let into our heart.

How Big is Your Monkey?

"After being clean for three years, I didn't think using would be a problem when I got out. But the very first party blew that illusion all to hell."

I remember a dude in a north Louisiana jail saying his drug habit was like Godzilla when he just had to stomp a few towns. Almost all of us are addicts in one way or another. Some joneses are minor, some super heavy...but they all eat our lunch if given half a chance. Usually our dependencies are the weakest links in our lives, the place where we are most vulnerable and fearful. Anyone wanting to leave the criminal justice system behind needs to honestly answer the following question: Was my arrest and captivity a result of an obsession that drove me to surrender control of myself? Yes or no.

If yes, the path to success after release will require us to do battle with that addiction. Dependency, by its very nature, takes control of what we do. It can be so powerful that we come to believe it has its own personality and strength apart from us, but this is not true. In fact addiction is part of the way we think! It's something **inside our heads** that we embrace to help us meet the demands of daily life, something we depend on to help "take the edge off." But it never gives us lasting relief. The price we pay for cheap thrills and quick relief is the energy we need to have a richer life.

Often we think such things as drugs, sex, alcohol, or gambling are our problem, but that's not true. Our real problem is whatever drives us to **surrender** to mood-altering behaviors. Whenever you find an action, item, feeling, or person you "can't live without," that is a clear danger sign! Take a close and honest look to see if your behavior is based on a positive choice or a negative obsession. Nothing in life should have so much power that we cannot enjoy life without it! The question is, "What can we do about it?"

Life Without a Crutch

"So what if booze and crack do fry my liver and turn my brain to rust? Everybody has to die of something!"

For me and thousands of ex-cons I've known, nothing is more deadly in the free world than being lost in one or more dependencies. Although we know something is hurtful, we often hold fast to our ways even if it kills us. Coming out of prison puts a lot of stress on a person. When emotions and events overpower us, we may seek relief through dope, a bottle, extreme sexual activity, hurting people, etc. But the cold fact is that drugs, etc., don't solve our problems. They only delay them for a very short period. The problems are still right there the next day, just waiting to pounce on us!

Coming out of a joint is the time when you need every little bit of yourself to cope and grow. The very last thing you need is another drain on your limited energy and resources. So look within yourself and find your pocket of addiction. If you can't function without a cup of coffee, smoke two packs of cigarettes a day, are obsessed over some person, have a serious eating problem, get lost in pornography, etc., it's time to do something about it! What is the goal here? **Freedom!**

You do not have to be a slave to a craving that destroys your dignity and self-worth. The idea that "once an addict, always an addict" is a cop out. You can learn to control and re-direct your mind and body. You may not be able to do it alone, but you **can** do it – that's a fact! Deal with it!

The burden is on you. Overcoming an addiction takes a lot of courage and hard work. It also takes a lot of help from people who understand what you're struggling with. Once you admit your problem, there is help available; you just need to reach out for it. *Life Without a Crutch* can aid you in understanding the power of addiction and finding help to overcome it. If you do nothing else to prepare yourself for future success, **get this book and read it cover to cover!**

Overcoming Major Barriers

Half In, Half Out

"Even though my mind knows I'm out, something inside me is still in that cage and it hasn't been able to shake free!"

If you've never lived it, it is impossible to explain what it's like to re-enter society right out of prison. Some compare it to waking up after a hundred-year sleep. First, you appreciate a lot of small things that others take for granted. One example is **privacy**, just being able to be alone, quiet, away from the endless noise and presence of others. And it's truly grand to be able to come and go as you need and want to. Even a walk in the park can be a real joy! So let it all soak in.

If you've spent five years surviving in a prison, then right after you get out it's natural to think and talk about your life behind bars. At first, prison memories and war stories are all you have to share with others. This is okay except that it blows most folks slam away and brings conversation to a dead stop! So try to grow more aware every time you do it and chill out whenever possible. Until you get over this, practice making "small talk" based on daily events. Even if this does seem sort of dull to you at first, that's where squares' heads are at! Use your insight, but spare folks the details of how and where you learned it.

Just as the adjustment to prison came in steps, so does return to the free world. A common and deadly trap for ex-cons and their families is trying to rebuild overnight. It's like thinking you can go from an empty lot to a skyscraper in a week. Lots of stress comes from expecting a magical, instant way to make everything wonderful. **The longer you were down, the longer it takes to put the puzzle together.** In fact, for a long time after release, you don't even know what the pieces look like or how to find them. Some of the pieces you need may not even exist. In this case, it can take you years to learn to make them. So you can't expect to feel comfortable in the world for quite a while. You need to be patient and determined to find your final way out of the maze!

Don't try to catch up on what you've missed; it cannot be done. You cannot re-live the time you've lost, any more than you can capture a river in a bucket. All of life is ahead of you, but it will come in small bites. Trying to "get it all now" is impossible. If you eat too much, your system cannot handle it. You just end up vomiting all over yourself. Be sure to study *99 Days and A Get Up* to get a good grip on the pace of your adjustment.

It normally takes a year or two before a person is more "here" than "there." It will depend on how much time you did, how old you are, and what came down during your stay. It takes a long time partly because the trip is so intense and because you have to slowly build a new way of living. With time and effort, prison becomes the past, just old history, as it is replaced with new, fresh experiences. The best way to put the pen behind you is to reach out into the world for positive energy, replacing the old with the new. Once again, this takes **time!**

If, after a few years, you find your mind is "still in the joint" or your anger continues to take control, be smart and seek professional counseling to help heal the wounds. If you don't, your out-of-control emotions will endanger you, your bonds with those you love, and possibly even your freedom.

The 60-Month Clock Begins

Remember that if a person remains arrest-free for five years after release, he or she is essentially out of danger. So if you carry yourself in ways which make this possible, you will not go back to prison. Instead, you will have achieved a solid, meaningful way of life, along with the rewards that come with it.

We will now review this critical five-year period in order to become better prepared for the ultimate success in your life following release.

The First Six Months

---

*"When you get out, life is like a roller-coaster
running wide open! There's no way to get off,
so you grit your teeth and hold on!"*

The first six to nine months after release are **wild!** It's like being on a roller-coaster running out of control. All you can do is hang on for dear life. This is true both for ex-prisoners and for those who have awaited their return. This period is full of turn-arounds, unexpected confusion and depression, childish delights, social rejections, and strange surprises. Many of the things you count on happening don't come to pass. And all too many things you prayed would miss you will come down on you like a load of bricks!

So this is a time for rapid adjustment of your hopes and plans. You can help keep your balance by taking pleasure in your new-found liberty and re-discovering some of the joys of just being alive! You can handle it, as long as you stay mentally prepared and keep a good sense of humor. Laugh at yourself!

It's also useful to **do daily attitude checks** to keep yourself on target. Look for problems, like unloading your emotions onto other people during stressful moments. Also give yourself credit for the progress you've made. Stay flexible and ready to adjust your plans. Don't let any problem overwhelm you or push you into dangerous behavior.

If you hold your feelings inside, you will finally explode. So do all you can to communicate what you think and feel to the people you care about. This doesn't mean having an outburst of negative emotions or complaining about your problems day after day. But it is critical to your well-being that you express your feelings honestly and openly. You may believe you're so different that no one can understand you, but you will find that people can often accept your sincerity and listen without passing judgment.

Also keep a sharp eye on how you treat those around you. It's not unusual to try to manipulate people or use the force of your body or will to keep them in line. This might have worked in the joint, but it is a sure kiss of death when you're trying to make or keep friends. You know you don't like to be used and abused. In fact, you view anyone who does so as an enemy. You can be sure that other people will feel the same way if you try to lean on them. And, by now, you should realize you need all the friends you can get!

Coming home can be very wonderful or quite deadly. Be careful not to bounce out of the pen into an addiction or emotional dependency – not just drugs or booze, but other extremes such as getting married your first month on the streets to someone you just met. Any of these escapes will end up becoming a new prison. And don't be

This is nothing new. After all, you've been treated like a throw-away for years. But now you are on the streets and feel you should be "free" to run your own show and have things your way.

However, this is never a simple matter. Ex-cons often come out of prison resenting anyone who tries to exercise power or authority over them. Many former prisoners walk around with a huge chip on their shoulders, quick to take offense at anything or anybody who resists their whims. In fact, they often over-react with strong emotions to situations that the average citizen deals with in a calm, effective way.

How you respond to "authority" and "people who just say NO" will have a major impact on your welfare. Automatic, get-in-their-face resistance to all external controls can be a real problem. After all, some authority is reasonable and must be dealt with. And, in most cases, the way people react to you is not a personal rejection of you but a response to the limits of reality. For example, an agency counselor cannot give you something he or she does not have or something that doesn't exist in the community.

So how do we tell the difference between "authority" which is reasonable and valid, and "opposition" which is unreasonable and just plain silly? Second, how do we, as ex-convicts, deal with being abused or intruded upon by idiots – the fools and jokers of the world?

To begin with, we expect to cope with reasonable authority figures such as our parole officer, employer, teachers, or certain family members. And there are people with whom we share authority and decisions, like our mates and friends. There are also people, like store clerks or receptionists, who are "just doing their jobs," even if we don't like the results.

But we shouldn't have to put up with some rude parking lot attendant who thinks he's running something. Still, before you jump out and bite this fool's ear off in front of a dozen witnesses, ask yourself a few questions. First, are you really reacting to the present situation or to something in your past? Is it in your best interest to get in this guy's face over trivial stuff? Is this really a valid issue or are you just looking for an excuse to unleash your anger? Are you exercising control over yourself? And, to be blunt, are **you** being a bigger idiot than he is? For many of us, this is the sad truth when we over-react with immediate and extreme hostility.

No matter how we feel about a situation, we must stay cool enough to recognize what's really happening and respond in a suitable way. By "suitable," I mean matching someone's action with our best possible response. A suitable response is one which leads to the most positive and constructive results. In order to respond suitably, we must be in control of our minds and emotions so that we can identify the best potential outcome and choose the most effective actions to achieve it.

Remember that a lot of "unimportant people" huff and puff just to feed their egos. It's like that in the joint and can be even worse on the streets. Dealing with a teenage drunk who thinks he's Superman, as an example, is nothing but a pain! But you must remind yourself that it isn't worth the price of a parole revocation to show him he can bleed. So be very careful: don't take everything personally! You don't have to act as absurd as he does. Let him find somebody who hasn't been to prison yet to break his face. You have far more important things to do. It really helps to remind yourself over shocked that many things have changed (*"Wow, there used to be a 20-story building here!"*). Most ex-cons who have been down five years or more cannot believe how fast things move out here. So it's essential to kick back, watch, listen, and learn.

Most people feel very helpless during the first six months to a year, but that will pass. You will get knocked down many times; this is a normal part of life even if you haven't been to jail or prison. It's okay just as long as you keep getting back up! It takes time, courage, and lots of work to make life as good as it can and should be. Every time things get **really** strange, just say to yourself, *"At least I'm not in the joint!"* No matter how rough it is at first, never doubt that **you can be a winner!**

Priest or Pirate?

"I felt as though the word 'CON' was branded right between my eyes for the whole world to see."

Anyone who has been convicted of a crime and sent to prison will have a negative social image, and this often leads to rejection on many levels. There are lots of citizens who will refuse to have anything to do with a "criminal." Being denied a job or a chance to improve just because of your record can be very frustrating. But no matter how much being rejected hurts your feelings, you need to learn to blow it off. Remember that fear and mistrust come with the rap sheet; they won't go away overnight just because you want them to.

We all know that people are quick to judge others. But don't let other people's opinions shake your sense of your own worth. Often their views are based on what they were taught as children, on cultural values, or selfish interests. They may be right and they may not. Your actual worth is based on your character and the results of what you think and do. Nothing more and nothing less.

It is better if people throw flowers at you rather than stones. Better they call you a hero rather than a villain. But no matter how others see you, the real issue is how you actually behave, in thought and action. Therefore, the only accurate labels are those which reflect the facts of your behavior. If you lie, you are a "liar." If you tell the truth, you are "an honest person." So your best chance of being defined as a "good person" comes from doing good deeds. Even if no one else is aware, the person who truly knows who and what you are is you.

Getting Pushed Around

"Everybody thinks they're running something – but usually it's nothing but their mouths!"

Day in and day out we interact with people. It's a give-and-take world. But let's face it: there will be lots of people who oppose you or refuse to give you your way.

and over that you are not responsible for what others do. But you are responsible for how you respond to them. Be the one sane person in a world of crazies!

Frankly, I found it very hard to put up with such trash. During my first five years out, I got off into more than a few wrecks that could have put me back behind bars for life. But I can see now that I was walking around with personal problems much bigger than the petty stuff people laid on me. In short, I was searching for an excuse to explode. And as you know, if you go looking for trouble, you will find it or it will find you.

Getting Settled

18 Months – A House of Cards

"Everything was going great! Then, without warning, my car blew up, my lady moved out, and I got fired for missing work...all in the same week! It seemed like I was better off in the joint."

For the first couple of years after release, everything is very fragile. Any big wind can come along and blow you away. Just about the time you get on top of your basic survival needs and think you've got something going for yourself, **KA-WHAM!** One little thing will go wrong and suddenly your house of cards comes tumbling down!

So this is a dangerous time. You haven't had a chance to save any resources to fall back on, so it's easy to be washed away. This is one reason ex-cons have to keep their game as tight as possible and not be shocked when one day, for no apparent reason, the bottom seems to fall out. I've watched it happen to me and many hundreds of people. Just keep in mind that it's all part of the maze; everyone has to live through it in one form or another. Despite the letdown, this is just another step, another phase.

It may seem that you're suddenly back where you started; you may even wonder "why bother?" But that is just the mood of the moment. It will pass. Think of it as a test of what you're made of. In fact it is a **temporary setback** – certainly it's not the end of the world. The only danger is if you give up and refuse to rebuild what you've lost.

In truth, by now you have a lot more going for you than when you hit the bricks, so just pull it back together and keep *cooking!* Don't let anything break your heart at this critical moment. This is part of your dues – reality teaching you not to depend on your possessions or anything beyond your control. You haven't lost yourself, **so deal with it!** The goal is to come out a bit wiser so it doesn't happen again.

24 Months – Facing the Unexpected

"My past and my future were like two people in the same skin…and they were total strangers!"

Two years or so have passed since exit. By now you can clearly see that much of what you focused on while down and right after release was trivial garbage or wishful thinking. Since then, reality has stomped your head in a few times and shown you how blind you were.

This is especially true with romances. Like many people, you may have used a relationship to keep you going while in prison and help you get a fresh start in the streets. But now your illusions are fading, attitudes are shifting, and you may feel trapped. You may want to stay, but feel you need to go. You hunger for security, but you also burn to be free to ride the midnight winds. Things feel very strange, but you can't put your finger on why or what to do about it.

At this point, many people are torn between the influence of the past and hopes for the future. We often try to "pull up," to find some stability and quality of life we've never had. At the same time we don't feel comfortable with our new ways; we're not really sure we fit into a good-citizen role. So we stay in touch with our old ways – trying to keep a foot in both worlds. But we don't have enough energy, time, and resources to go forward and backward at the same time. And when we try to go both ways, we cancel ourselves out and end up standing still!

Do everything possible to stay stable during this confusing time. You are not the old person you used to be and you aren't yet the new person you want to become. You are in between, which makes you feel a lot of stress and even guilt. Calm down and look within yourself to get a clear picture of who you are **today** and what steps you need to take **tomorrow**. Don't get hung up on who you used to be, what you don't have yet, or what you wish the future to hold. Take care of the business that's right in front of you. And think carefully before you make any decisions about major changes in your life. You don't want to build your future on something that could be a passing whim.

If you think you're going to blow it, get help to sort things out and work through this period of confusion. And I don't mean by consulting a fifth of Jack Daniels or a bag of home grown pot. Look for someone you respect who can see things more clearly than you; it will help you get your balance back. As you go through these growing pains, it's natural to hit the wall at times. What's important is that you learn to handle it in a way that results in progress and pride!

30 Months – Critical Choices

*"You make your own heaven and you make your own hell…
with 95% of it being inside your own head!"*

It's been about 30 months since release and lots of good things have come together. You have lived through the shock of release, pulled together your basic survival needs, overcome some major hassles, sorted out a lot of conflict, and begun to feel a part of the world. Great! You've come a long way, paid a high price, and have good reason to feel pride. Now it's time to confront a real moment of truth that will make or break you.

In prison all you wanted was to **survive** and **get out**. After release all you wanted was to **survive** and **stay out**. Things were hard but clear: you had to cope! Now that you are not totally driven by the after-shock of prison, you face some **critical choices**.

Daily life begins to place more and more petty burdens on you – stuff like car repairs, taxes, and school clothes for your kids. There is no place to hide. Your fate rests in **your** hands. You handle it or it eats you. No more promises to your family, parole officer, or yourself. Excuses don't cut it. Where you are right now is where you've said for years you wanted to be: in charge of your fate. Every day offers a crossroads: "In-Control Land" to the right, "Out-of-Control Land" to the left.

What is it going to be? Look life straight in its bloodshot eye, or retreat into chaos? What's your choice? At this point some folks are still trying to play both sides of the fence. But they become increasingly spread out, way too vulnerable. It only takes one serious slip-up and you're screwed. While other people can afford to waste their lives and send themselves to hell, you have already been there! Take advantage of the dues you've paid. Make a commitment to do **whatever it takes** to have maximum control over your life.

No matter which road you take, each has its own set of rules, risks, and responsibilities. But before you choose the outlaw side, make yourself **remember**. Look back at how it feels to be chained up and treated like gorilla snot. Recall how it felt when your best friend turned state's evidence against you. Keep in mind how your father died while you were down and you couldn't even go to the funeral. And next time you slip, you might run the risk of catching life as a habitual criminal. Make yourself remember!

Ask yourself, "Is there anything in the pen I need to go back to learn? Did I miss something last time around? Is there any future in playing the outlaw role? Do I want to die in a cage?"

Don't let anything or anyone distort your vision. Being responsible for yourself is hard work – **very** hard – and often not very exciting. But each new day that you make the choice to control your life is a step away from slavery toward freedom. You have earned your pride and self-respect, because you are making great progress. **Don't give up!**

36 Months – The Three-Year Itch

*"When you finally get the Man's boot off your neck,
you tend to go crazy with relief. I got real cocky and
was ready to take on the whole world."*

There is something about being out about three years that is very weird and potentially disastrous. It's probably a mixture of things. By now you have some really good stuff going for yourself and you're determined to get more out of life than just survival. Also, you have more energy and part of you is **bored to the bone**. Plus, you have begun to forget just how bad it really was to be a slave and treated like you're ugly and stupid. You may even be thinking that your success in the free world has made you invisible and invincible.

Be careful. Keep yourself humble – or something is going to come along and kick your butt loose from the rest of your body. And that's an absolute fact! Dig it: **being free does not mean you can run loose and loud**. Around the three-year mark, one of two things happens: you get a close call that leaves you breathless, dizzy, and thankful. Or you go down again (prison, nut house, hospital, graveyard, whatever). No kidding, when you catch yourself getting real bold and starting to run hot, watch out because you are riding for a fall.

Settle down now and be very, *very* careful. You've come too far and paid too high a price to blow it over some nickel-and-dime trash. This is a time to hold your head up, do everything you can to make **good choices**, and finally realize that in fact **you can make it!** The best way to avoid the three-year trap is to take a deep breath, clean up your act, re-dedicate yourself to personal growth, and focus your extra energy on turning your dreams into reality.

You have made excellent progress! The secret here is to put your growing energy and intensity to ever greater use. Continue to seek better ways to handle yourself, in thought and action. Branch out into more educational, social, and cultural activities in your community. Take a night class, study self-defense, take up a new hobby, improve your job skills. This is a very sensitive time: **keep on moving forward!**

40 Months – Don't Rock the Boat

*"Do not be consumed by your own fire!
Settle down, keep your balance, and begin
to really enjoy your freedom."*

By now you have successfully endured the major hardships of life after prison. You should feel a lot of satisfaction, because you've held onto your commitment to make it happen. You've made a big investment, and you can actually taste and touch the positive results. At this point, you don't want to lose it – it feels too damned good! You never had that when you were ripping and running! You know now, without question, that what you want and need is in the free world, not in a concrete zoo.

I'll be the first to admit that the so-called "free world" leaves a lot to be desired, but **keep your vision clear!** No matter how dull and dumb square life may seem, it has to be better than lying up on Christmas Eve in an ice-cold tomb of concrete and steel. Living a solid, productive, rewarding life doesn't mean you have sold out. You've simply wised up to the fact that your life is what you make it.

By now you know there are trade-offs you must make for the things you want and need; everything has a price. Clearly a lot of sweat is required to put up with the endless details of daily living. But you also have proof that taking control of your welfare really pays off. You don't work on blind faith anymore. So when you get discouraged, sit down and have a heart-to-heart talk with yourself. Just look at the progress you've made – **just look!** Your efforts have earned you a new life of freedom and self-reliance.

Still, you sure are sick of the constant ups and downs of the roller-coaster you've been on. You want more stability, even though stable living may not fit into your picture of yourself. Some hot shots might think the idea of being "stable" is just plain silly. But not you – you've been rebuilding your life from scratch and you know better.

Over the years since release, you haven't just been sitting in a dark corner, playing a dull, square game. Not at all! You are not the same person who hit the streets confused, frustrated, and angry. You have been living, growing, meeting new people, expanding your mind, and discovering the world as never before. And along the way there have been rewards – events and feelings that have encouraged you and given you reason to persist against all odds.

You've come a long way; you've earned the right to have more quality and comfort in your life. And the way to put it there is to continue growing. By this time you know a lot about what you want in your life, work, and relationships. So keep working to improve in these areas! **Focus** your energy on getting yourself where you want to be. Improve your job skills so you won't be the first to get laid off. Set up a savings plan so that when something goes wrong it won't knock over your whole deck of cards. Work on solving problems in your relationships before they blow up in your face.

At the same time, you must realize that stable living does not mean things will always stay the same. No matter how stable you are, change will still occur. This is just the way life is. You can control some of the shifts but not all. The solution is to improve your ability to deal with the unexpected curves that reality throws at you. Your greatest source of security will be a calm confidence that you can cope with any obstacles you run into.

So think positive, hold your head up, and take another step forward. Be proud of what you have built, have faith in what you are going to achieve – and be thankful you are not going to die in a solitary cell with nothing but roaches for friends!

48 Months – Couch Potato Boogie

"When you don't have to be lean and mean any more,
it's way too easy to kick back and get fat! A BIG trap!"

You never wanted the experience of going to prison or having to build a new life after you got out. Thus everything you've done so far has been out of *sheer* necessity. Looking back over the last four years, you will see a long path of efforts just to endure.

But mere survival is not the issue anymore. You have done a great job of dealing with the panic and crisis that came with life after prison. Now that the edge is off and the memory of the pain has eased up, many people are tempted just to coast. And if you aren't careful you can turn into a big, fat, lazy slug! Beware: life doesn't stop here!

There's no reason to simply settle for life in a rut – even a comfortable middle-class rut. Having what it takes to get by isn't enough! The new challenge is to protect all that you have built and keep moving forward. It's time to reach for the next gear. From this point on, you can aspire to improved **balance** in your life and continued **progress**.

You are now very close to the door of the maze. Freedom is in sight! Recommit yourself to whatever it takes to break free from the past. Up to now, events have forced you to focus on surviving one crisis after another. Now the crises are more infrequent. For the first time you can afford to aim far more energy and attention forward than you do backward. But it's up to you to keep on pushing; you will have to supply the focus. Strive to keep your mind and actions steady while having the courage and dedication to advance into the unknown. Are you going to settle for just getting over the past, or will you use this as a wonderful chance to make your life the way you've always dreamed it could be?

Life in the world offers so many more choices than you had in prison or in the reconstruction period after release. But you need new levels of self-discipline and courage to make living truly full and rewarding. Surely you haven't struggled so hard just to become a beer-drinking, TV-zapped couch potato.

It seems strange that, when you've already overcome so many obstacles, you need a fresh supply of strength and willpower to keep from getting lulled to sleep by your own success! Now that you have something going for yourself, you also have something to lose. At this point every ex-con has a new choice: to make life sweet or to screw up big-time. You don't want to blow what you have already achieved, but beyond that...you must take full advantage of this chance to live life to the fullest. You have dedicated your life to finding this door to the future. Now it's time to open it and step through.

54 Months – Facing Your Demons

> *"That there is a devil, I have no doubt. But is it outside trying to get in, or inside trying to get out?"*

Your growth and maturity are calling on you to tackle the **causes** behind some of your life-long problems. These are issues that go back to your roots, perhaps to childhood – very deep concerns you've never had the time, motivation, or ability to confront. You are ready to move beyond a survival holding pattern, but you keep running into some old walls, time after time! You can no longer permit them to stand in your way. Achieving escape velocity demands that you face these long-term barriers.

These barriers are like a group of demons that have been chewing on us for as long as we can remember. Even before any of us became prisoners of the State, we were prisoners of our own fears, self-images, and patterns of living that blocked our quest for peace and happiness. Beyond our reach, these ghosts still haunt us, affecting our interactions with ourselves and the world. Each time we think we're ready to step forward into a new life, our demons hook into our guts and snatch us back.

You've arrived at a very critical point in your quest for freedom. No longer can you simply accept being blown with the wind. It is time to turn about and face the invisible forces which command you! This is your only hope for gaining mastery over your fate. You now have the opportunity to begin fixing major parts of yourself that have never, ever worked. Not just repainting the front door, but re-leveling the very foundation of your being!

Such deep, hard work is best faced with the ongoing help of a professional counselor. This is not someone who will manipulate, control you, or mess with your head. A counselor is a guide who can help you look at your thoughts, feelings, and actions from a different perspective so that you can start to work through rather than around your past! Here is where you begin to give the word "freedom" its true meaning in your life. You don't have to be trapped in the past just because "that's the way things have always been." With courage, persistence, and guidance from a wise teacher or counselor, you can free yourself from past limits.

Although this may have seemed impossible before, your years of hard work and growth have made you much stronger, wiser, and more balanced. Therefore, it's time to get serious about mastering the forces which lead to **quality of life**.

You may need to learn how to set reasonable limits on yourself and others, how to tell the difference between "enough" and "too much." You may decide your self-image as a loser needs to go. Or maybe it's time to overcome your guilt, fear, insecurity, or inability to love and be loved – whatever it is that has kept you chained to unhappiness and failure. This rebuilding of your own foundation is the most intense form of personal growth. Your progress has earned you the right to get past the icing and deal with the cake.

60 Months – A Five-Year Victory

"Five long years of resisting the urge to dig my old .45 out of the sock drawer! But I can see now it was a wise decision!"

Every new day of freedom is a victory because each brings with it a new chance to grow and prosper. But some points of progress are more special and rewarding in our lives than others. When you hit five years of arrest-free living, it is time to celebrate big time! To get this far means you have cleared 75% of the hurdles to success. More important, you have, at long last, found the door to the maze. You've actually made it!

How do you know it has really taken place? Is there a crack of thunder? Do you get a letter from the President? Does somebody give you a new Cadillac convertible? Most important, what does it feel like to know you have finally fought your way out?

Obviously each person will feel it in different ways. I can only share with you what I personally felt when it happened to me. The following is my word picture of the experience I had when I realized I had finally exited the maze. Perhaps it will help you understand why this is a goal worth working and waiting for.

"It had been a long, hot, nasty 4th of July running northwest into a merciless New Mexico sun. Thirteen hours on the back of my 1946 Harley chopper (*The Hand Grenade*) with the rigid frame chipping teeth as I'd go airborne over train trestles.

The traffic was horrid rolling up the slope of the southern Rockies. For miles I'd been stuck behind an old logging truck as it lumbered around tight mountain curves. The driver refused to let me pass, and I was blind with rage, determined to get around him or die in the process. As we started up a steep incline, I dropped into third and punched it. I roared past him and hit fourth just as I swooped over the crest.

Suddenly the sky exploded into a vast sunset of untold power and beauty. A million muted shades from mauve to aquamarine stretched across the limitless sky. It took my breath away and I laughed way down inside. I was finally free!

As the sun slowly settled into the horizon, the shadow of my bike reached out beside me, dancing among the fence posts along the road. In a heart beat, the first sweet, cool, sweet breezes of evening brought a rush of well-being that dissolved my fatigue, soothed my anger, and filled my heart with peace.

At the bottom of the next valley, I pulled off onto a dirt road and shut down in a pocket of trees beside a small mountain lake. As my ears opened to the sounds of the forest, I could hear the chatter of birds seeking their nests for the night. The water was a smooth mirror, rippled only by the occasional strike of a small fish. Here, totally alone in this quiet, private spot, I understood that all the struggles and day-to-day hassles I had endured in a cage were just the price I paid for the joy and magic of this instant.

It was in that instant I realized that it took all the pain and suffering of prison to make me who I was. It was all that madness and isolation that had prepared my heart for the majesty of this enchanted moment. This private peace was what I'd dreamed of for 10 years. Now here it was – and everything was **totally okay**. It was then that I knew for the first time I was truly a free man!"

The Rewards of Success

Step Right Up

"Look within your heart for the key to your fate. It is there."

What is it you want from your life? The path I suggest leads to three things: **maximum liberty, rewarding personal ties, and the satisfaction of life well lived**. But these are only words on paper until you reach down within yourself and create a vision of the person you wish to become.

My purpose throughout this book has been to strengthen your resolve to walk through fire to achieve the personal growth that will enable you to reach five years of arrest-free living. Yet I have no special power to change the way you think and act: only you have that. All I can really do is appeal to your better judgment and desire to lead the best life possible.

Vague promises of better times will not alter your way of looking at the world. And just because I have learned to value life and my place in it doesn't mean I can convince you to do the same. It is totally up to you! At this instant, you may be longing for a way out of the pit...or simply too tired and hopeless to believe you can truly "stand up." Either way, it is your right to choose. All I can do is point the way: "Better Times – Step Right Up!"

If, as you read this, you are still an inmate existing from moment to moment, your mind caught up in that sick, tiny world, it will be hard for you even to imagine the rush of achieving a life beyond the criminal justice system. It might be easier to understand how an astronaut feels floating in space than to imagine the type of freedom and opportunity I'm talking about. So much time and distance may stand between you and this level of freedom that it seems like a cruel joke to talk about being five years free.

This is understandable, because the journey from release to success in the free world is still a total unknown for you. You may have stumbled so many times in the past you think success is impossible. In fact, you may not have a clue as to what the hell I'm talking about! In fact, for someone who has never experienced it, the rich rewards of a life full of freedom and achievement may be beyond imagining.

How, then, do I convince you to invest your mind, body, and heart in something you cannot see, touch, smell, or otherwise know? I can only hope that when I tell you how good I feel about the changes I've made in my life – and the changes I have watched others make over the years – you will believe that such powerful and rewarding changes can also occur in your life.

Creating a life style that enables five years of arrest-free living is a huge challenge. Yet it enables a total makeover of who and what you are! By dedicating yourself to 60 full moons of serious effort, you will, slowly but surely, heal the scars of the past, replacing them with health, hope, and achievement. And from this come pride, dignity, and peace of mind. It is available to you…**but you must want it more than anything else in the world!**

Becoming an EX Ex-Con

"I refuse to have my FBI number cut into my grave stone!"

Let's say you have in fact made it for five years without being flushed by your attitude and actions or by some gung-ho cop. Still, you may carry the negative label of "criminal" in your own mind. After years of isolation and ridicule, you may have bought into the idea that you really were a worthless reject. This negative identity can lead to public rejection and limited opportunities in the community. And it can have an equally profound effect on the way you see yourself.

But now, after five years of work, faith, and positive changes, that negative self-image is just useless baggage that keeps you a prisoner of the past. At this point in your life, you can shed the label of "criminal" like a snake sheds its skin. Just look at the strides you've made, the lessons you've learned. You are not the same person who stumbled out of the joint five years ago! By now you not a "criminal" or "ex-con," but simply a "human being."

Being a convict is a tragic waste of time and energy. Why would anyone want to hang onto the experience and die an "ex-con"? Granted you have a criminal record and face problems with employment and housing…but these are external conditions, not an identity. You don't have to accept the idea that you are some kind of social trash or public menace. Never forget that you have made great progress in efforts to outgrow past mistakes. And you can continue this development in the years ahead. You do this by slowly replacing "criminal" thoughts and acts with health, growth, and prosperity. Every step is major progress!

The only way to really beat the system and become truly free is to let go of a negative past and embrace a positive future. You are well on your way. Focus all your energy now on making the future rich, full, and free! It can be done and you can do it!

Inside the Circle

"To be within the Circle of Life means coming into a sense of harmony with yourself, loved ones, community, and the whole of creation!"

The day of conviction, we were officially kicked out of the circle of social acceptance, labeled as **outcasts**, and exiled to the Land of Castaways. After that, many of us felt "alone to the bone," completely cut off, totally isolated. And the period of captivity encouraged us to take the next step into self-isolation, becoming a stranger even to ourselves. This is the ultimate trap of the maze. Therefore, one of the most important steps in leaving the maze is to renew our contact with ourselves and re-enter the circle of humanity.

When you first came out of the joint, you may have seen the world as "the enemy" and gone through a period of telling everyone to go straight to hell. Your attitude may have been, *"So they don't want me? Well, who needs 'em?!"* If so, it was in part because your anger and hate prevented you from bonding with others or being part of the world you live in. But after you've been out five years, you have some real successes under your belt, most of all that you are still here in the free world. You have made many adjustments in order to get along in society and have some different ideas about who you are and what you want out of life. In fact, you are now a contributing member of the community. A trustworthy neighbor, employee, and friend.

But your awareness may lag behind reality. You may still feel an echoing emptiness surrounding you in the midst of a crowd. If so, now is the time to let go of that lone-wolf identity. You don't need it as protection any longer. You are a unique and important person who has made a place for yourself in the world. It is safe to start letting down your walls and re-connecting with the people around you.

This is a gradual process and one that is different for each individual. If you don't know how to begin, that's a good reason to get some guidance from a professional counselor. You can use the help, not because you are sick, but because you are ready to get healthier.

At some point, you will find you just don't need so many defenses anymore. You will realize that there is a gateway through your walls and you have the key. Maybe it will come to you in the quiet way it came to me.

"In prison I pulled back, totally and completely, from everyone and everything. I identified with the label "single O," a loner's loner. For many years this condition continued in the streets. No matter where I was, who I was with, or what we were doing, I was alone! My isolation was both my shelter and my tomb. The hard part was learning to trust!

Gradually I met some truly fine people, and over time began to feel more comfortable, more 'there' when other people were around. Last week we had some people over for dinner. As we sat around the table, it hit me that I was part of the group – I actually fit! I wasn't just sitting back watching what was happening; I was an accepted part of this circle of friendship. It was like a great weight t lifted from my back, as though my soul could finally breathe. Far more than just being out of prison, I was truly home!"

Life Beyond the Maze

> *"Instead of just living day-to-day, it's time
> to get ahead of the game."*

Up until now most of your energy has been spent trying to overcome your past and exit the maze. Survival and damage control have been the major concerns. In short, most of your attention has been on what you're moving away **from** rather than what you're moving **to**. Now, with most survival issues in check, you can look forward, into the **future!** More and more you can let go of the past and shift your attention to new, fresh ways to think and live.

What awaits you on the other side of the maze? As you shift into a higher gear, you begin to reap some of the rewards for all your years of serious work, faith, and patience. At this point you can begin to pursue some long-term goals that will bring you greater stability and tremendous satisfaction.

Shop the fall sales for things you'll need next spring. Plan for the overseas trip that you once lay in a cell and dreamed about. Look at what it will take to buy a house rather than renting. Think about what you would need to do to pursue a career change or to start your own business. Now is the time to look at your truly long-range plans and decide how to make them real.

And as you continue to improve your own life, **also think about what you can do to improve the world around you**. As long as you were fighting to survive, you didn't have anything left over to share with the world. You couldn't give what you didn't have. But now you have some physical, financial, and emotional security. Granted it's not what you want it to be yet, but you can now afford to give a little of yourself to the welfare of others. You have personal skills, a great deal of insight into life, and a powerful ability to focus your energy on a goal and make it happen. These are talents that can make a positive difference in your community.

So consider dedicating some of your resources to solving problems that are greater than your own life. Find an issue that needs work and means something to you, and decide to help make things better. This commitment to making the world a better place may be the most rewarding thing you will ever do. I know it has been for me.

The more you apply and focus yourself, the more power and control you will have over yourself and everything around you. This will lead to ever greater security, comfort, and quality of life, and to honest self-respect. Now that you have reached this point of achievement, you don't have to walk around looking at the ground anymore. You can look up at the stars!

Freedom, progress, and pride are no accident. **You've earned them!**

7

Advice for Families of Offenders

by Louis W. Adams, D.Min.

B EING THE FAMILY member or the loved one of a public offender results in countless problems and burdens which no one wants or is born knowing how to handle. Many social, emotional, spiritual, and financial difficulties arise when you become involved in the criminal justice system. At times, you may feel lost in these difficult and unexpected concerns.

In order to cope, it helps to know some of the basic problems and universal experiences people face during the correctional experience. One encouraging fact that helps survival and growth is the **predictable nature of the experience.** Many of the events and resulting challenges affect almost everyone who becomes involved. Although knowing what is to come does not make it simple or easy, it does improve your preparation and increase your confidence to handle the events in the most effective way possible.

Dealing With Loss

"The day of sentencing a big part of me died."

Family members and loved ones of persons caught up in the criminal justice system are going to have many of the same experiences the offender does. But they are also called on to endure feelings and events unknown to the inmate. While some of these emotional and social changes are similar to things people face in daily life, others are unique to the correctional process. At the heart of these experiences is one central issue – the sense of loss.

Personal Factors

First, you lose the physical presence and daily contact with the incarcerated person. Even though you may not have approved of their behavior, you were used to their presence and it comes as a shock when they suddenly vanish. He or she is no longer around to support you or "bug" you, as the case may be. You lose your personal interaction with that person. It may even feel as though a part of your body has been cut away.

You also lose the role they played in the family and other groups to which they belonged. That role might include financial, emotional, and/or spiritual contributions the loved one made through normal daily activities. Even if the person had become a drain on you, you will still miss having him or her involved with you from day to day.

Second, you have probably lost the person you always believed your loved one to be. You may have often said to them, *"You will end up in big trouble if you don't change what you're doing."* But you still believed and hoped that something would change before your loved one really did get into trouble. Their arrest, conviction, and imprisonment destroyed this belief and hope!

Your belief and hope have often been a very important part of your own values, goals, and expectations. Having them come to an abrupt end is experienced as a deep and painful "loss," a major event in your life. No one is ever really ready to confront such a significant loss. It will be felt as a loss even though the overall situation with the loved person has not been perfect or really satisfying. And when you experience a loss as "significant," it is natural for you to grieve that loss.

Grief is Natural

When a loved one is incarcerated, grief is a natural, human response. It includes any or all of a series of feelings which must be accepted and dealt with. The order in which these feelings are experienced may vary with each person.

The first feeling most people have is **shock**. It may be sensed as an absence of feeling, a kind of numbness or emptiness, rather than a sharp feeling like anger, betrayal, or pain. You may feel as if something is gone from your gut, like there is a hole there; you may feel light-headed; you may feel that you are not quite connected with your immediate world; or you may feel a combination of all of these. The onset of such feelings can be very disturbing. If you don't have any of the above reactions, you may feel nothing at all, and this absence of feeling can also be upsetting.

Confusion often follows or comes with the initial shock. But don't let the confusion, the absence of feeling, or the onset of strong negative feelings distort your sense of reality. This kind of reaction is not unusual; it is quite natural. Parts of the body, mind, or emotions sometimes shut down for a while. This protects you from being overwhelmed by unexpected, traumatic, and dreaded events. In this sense, shock may be helpful by acting as a temporary shield to protect you.

You may also defend against a trauma by trying to **deny** that the terrible event happened. This **often** occurs while you are in a state of shock. For example, when you first learn of your loved one's crime or incarceration, you may deny (or fervently hope) that what has happened simply isn't true. You keep hoping you will wake up and find the dreaded event was only a dream (well, maybe a nightmare). You may, against all evidence, continue to hope that it is all a giant mistake. But you will not wake up! It is not a mistake. What happened really **did** happen and you will have to accept it as true.

A state of shock does not usually last very long. But the denial of what happened may go on for days, weeks, months, or in some cases for years. No matter how natural or useful the denial is at first, you need to come out of the shock and denial. The sooner you can get yourself going again, the quicker you can start to be effective in handling your life and the situation you are facing.

Anger

"I just get so filled with rage at the whole situation!"

Once the numbness and denial of shock have passed, it is very common for a person to feel anger, lots of anger! You may feel **anger** toward your loved one because their actions caused the pain and problems which you now have to face. The anger can be very intense, especially if your loved one ignored your warnings and pleading to stop what they were doing. Your anger may be directed toward the police, the courts, an attorney, or toward "them." You will probably feel anger at times toward any or all of these sources, plus others.

Having angry feelings toward things and people outside yourself has its own set of problems with which you must deal. But anger is not confined just to outside objects or other persons. There is a very high probability that your anger will be turned back on yourself – in the end if not at first. This is a form of guilt, a self-blaming process. You may tell yourself such things as, "If I had been smart enough, good enough, persuasive enough, strong enough, worked hard enough, had knowledge enough, or paid attention to the signs of trouble sooner, I could have prevented all this from happening."

While there can be some truth in these criticisms, none of them is totally true. It is not useful to go on criticizing yourself indefinitely. Whenever you get angry or overly critical of yourself, and keep these feelings focused on yourself for a period of time, **depression** will set in. This is a fundamental rule of the life process.

Depression

"I could hardly drag myself out of bed; if it hadn't been
for feeding the kids, I wouldn't have bothered to face the day."

Depression is one of the most difficult parts of the grief experience. It is hard because it uses up so much of your emotional, psychic, spiritual, and physical energy. You will likely feel very bad, drained of all energy and initiative. Or you may feel flat, or just plain empty and hopeless.

You will probably fuss at yourself about various "failures" you have had both past and present. For example, you may feel guilty and tell yourself that you did not do the "right things" to prevent your loved one from being incarcerated. You may have tried hard to correct the behavior pattern your loved one was following, but your efforts did not help.

You may feel you bungled and did not get them the right kind of help. You may feel that all of your decisions during this ordeal were wrong and that this is why your loved one is incarcerated and you are in so much pain. You may feel your total life is a failure; not only have you failed your loved one, you may also believe that you have failed as a person throughout your life. This feeling is especially common among parents of prisoners.

If you pay attention to these failure messages and come to believe them, your confidence in yourself may be badly shaken and undermined. If you lose confidence in yourself, you will probably doubt your ability to make good decisions. You may therefore avoid making decisions altogether. And this is **not** a time to quit making decisions, no matter how difficult your choices seem to be.

Another reason that decisions are hard to make is because you don't have enough energy. The energy you once used to make decisions is now being used to deal with the depression. You simply don't have as much energy available to deal with the normal tasks and decisions of everyday living, let alone deal with any major decisions about the incarcerated person and your own affairs. You may find that you don't make decisions as easily or as effectively as you once did.

Even simple tasks do not get done as easily or as well as before. You have only a certain amount of energy available to deal with all of life's tasks. So when you use more of your energy to deal with your depression, less will be available for doing all the other things you have to do, such as making decisions. Your efficiency in dealing with life will suffer.

When you notice that you are less efficient, you may start to doubt your ability to do anything well. This in turn may cause you to fuss at yourself for your lack of ability. If this happens, you become more depressed and will doubt yourself even more. When you are caught in this depressed state of mind, everything around you can seem like quicksand. Every effort you make will seem to pull you down further into depression and ineffectiveness. You may even use this experience to prove to yourself that you are incompetent as a person.

At the same time, you will likely get more and more requests from your loved one to do things and solve problems. As these demands pile up, you will feel frustrated, and this can make you feel more depressed. You may get very tired and angry at the demands being made on you. No matter what you do, it seems to be not "enough," not "effective," not "right," or it turns out to be irrelevant or unnecessary. And when you do all these things for your loved one, you don't seem to have any energy left to do things for yourself.

When your anger and frustration reach a certain level, you will probably "dump" it. You may dump it on your incarcerated loved one, other family members, friends, your lawyer, the jailers, the judge, prison employees, the parole board or anyone else who happens to be handy. Of course, dumping anger and stress on others will not be helpful to you or your loved one. Neither will the added depression caused by the dumping. Often it just increases your own sense of frustration and helplessness.

Trying to endure levels of stress or pain beyond your limits can result in a physical or emotional illness. In this situation, you may feel so overwhelmed that you think you cannot hang on and simply want to give up! But this is not a positive solution; the situation won't go away even if you do give up. You will get greater relief by learning healthy ways to overcome depression and stress.

Other Feelings

Other feelings may also overcome you. You may feel shame, because your loved one has been labeled a "criminal." You may fear being **embarrassed** if co-workers or members of your church find out your loved one is in prison. And it is not uncommon for children of prisoners to be ridiculed by others at school or in the neighborhood. To make things worse, at times family members will reject other members because they continue to stand by an inmate. One or more of these things can cause you to isolate yourself from your friends or members of your family.

You may feel guilt, because you didn't prevent this from happening or because you "failed" to inspire your loved one to be a better person. You might also feel guilty because, at first, you were relieved that the uncertainty of the pre-trial activities was over. You may tell yourself that feeling relieved when someone dear to you is incarcerated is just "not right." Along with all of the above, you will probably feel **frustrated and powerless** simply because you have little or no control over what is happening.

You may experience any or all of these feelings in any order or several at a time. You may feel **overwhelmed** with them and think you are really losing control of yourself – maybe going crazy. This can increase your anger and guilt because you view yourself as inadequate to handle the load.

Sometimes the situation gets too "heavy" to bear, and you will walk (or run) away from it. When this happens, it may be that your mind and body are protecting you from an overload. Sometimes it is helpful to exit the stress of the moment and "hide" for a while. This lets you recover your balance and your perspective. Then you can return to the battle refreshed.

Such an act does not mean you are a weak or bad person or that you are uncaring, disloyal, or selfish. If you choose to do this to get recharged, don't let anyone put you on a guilt trip for deserting the battle. It is simply one way you can survive when you have reached the outer limits of your endurance.

However, if this happens often, or you do not get back into taking care of essential "business" within a reasonable time, it is a sign of danger for your health and future. It is time for you to seek outside help because you are probably running away from things you will have to face at some point. Putting them off will not make them go away.

Sometimes the troublesome feelings may go away for a while. You believe that you have, at last, gotten over your grief and depression. Then something happens, perhaps during a visit with your loved one, and the grief feelings return stronger than before. This, too, may make you think you're going crazy. Although very unpleasant, this is not particularly unusual. Feelings may come and go many times during the course of your grief. Even as you begin to move back into a more normal life pattern, these feelings – especially periods of depression, anger, and apathy – may return.

When the depressed feelings are strong, you may decide that nothing is really important. You may not care about anything and may do little or nothing. In more intense moods of depression, you may feel life is not worth living and there is no use in trying. In fact, you may get to the point where you believe that nothing good can happen, either now or in the future.

Even after your life is almost back to normal and you seem to be coping well with all your problems, you may have a recurrence of these feelings of depression. Even if this happens to you several times, do not despair. There is hope!

Fighting Depression

Depression Can be Overcome

"I didn't think I could ever enjoy going fishing without Henry, but I'm glad I tried it. I missed him, but I had a good time. And I felt more like coping with things when I got home."

Depression keeps you weak and helpless by telling you that you have no energy to do anything. It may cause your sleep to be disturbed so you feel even more tired. Your apathy may increase. Messages of hopelessness may become very, very strong and hard to resist. But do not give up! Depression can be overcome. It is not easy, but it is possible.

You start overcoming depression by making yourself do things even when you don't think you can. For example, you must **make yourself** go to work, clean the house, keep the car running well, spend time with other people. If you have trouble sleeping, do not lie in bed; get up and do those long-neglected chores you hate so much. After you do this once or twice, you may find you will go to sleep in order to avoid doing the things you hate to do!

Many people report that the hardest part of this task is making themselves do things that they used to enjoy doing. No matter how difficult this may be, you must make yourself do it. If you start doing these things and you make yourself get involved with caring people, you will be surprised to find that your energy has increased and your interest in life is vibrant again.

It is also important to stop doing things that aren't helpful or necessary, like smoking, drinking, overeating, neglecting personal appearance and hygiene, or second guessing all your decisions. Such activities have no benefit, either short- or long-term. Therefore, do not waste your precious energy on them.

Instead, do the things that take care of necessary business and help you relax. These will give you both short- and long-term benefits. Most people know what to do to take care of business, but often don't know how to relax. If you don't know how to relax, then now is the time to learn. Activities that relax you may also be fun. After you learn them, be sure you don't block yourself from doing them. In our society, people often believe it is "bad" to relax and have fun when a loved one is in prison, sick, or in trouble. Get this thought out of your mind. It is not useful or helpful.

Part of any person's responsibility is to take genuine care of his or her own physical, mental, emotional, and spiritual health. Taking care of necessary business is fundamental to this task. But relaxing and having fun are also an important part of this responsibility. When you relax and have fun, your self-esteem and self-confidence will grow. You will feel refreshed and able to use your energy more effectively. And when you feel competent and confident in yourself, the help you provide your loved one will be more effective.

Protect Yourself

"I found myself doing time day-for-day with my son,
but I got so miserable I was no help to him or me.
I had to shake myself out of it or go under."

A prisoner cannot come and go at will nor participate in the events of daily life. But the fact that your loved one is locked up does not mean you should be cut off from the world as well. You are not the one sentenced to prison. It does the prisoner absolutely no good for you to sit in a corner and sulk and brood until they are released.

However, a prison inmate can be very selfish. Your loved one may, in fact, expect you to suffer and brood in isolation just as they do. An inmate may not understand that you have the right to your own life – a calm, happy, normal, and healthy life – even if he or she is unable to have one. The prisoner may not realize that your help will be more useful and effective if you are feeling confident and satisfied about yourself.

Don't be caught off guard if your loved one criticizes or attacks you for doing things for fun and relaxation. It is not unusual for an inmate to accuse you of not caring, of being unfaithful or disloyal, etc., because you have been doing something fun. Don't let such criticism throw you! There is no reason to feel guilty about it, even if your loved one tries to make you feel guilty. Remember, you must keep your own emotional, spiritual, mental, and physical health in good order. This will help you keep your self-esteem and confidence high.

Relaxation and fun are part of your most important task – **to take care of yourself**. It is absolutely essential that you accomplish this task. And ultimately, it is one of the most helpful things you can do for your loved one. There is nothing to be gained by staying locked in your grief and agony. If you are not keeping yourself physically, mentally, emotionally, and spiritually healthy, you will not be as effective in helping your loved one, no matter how hard you try.

Accept Your Limits

Do not expect too much of yourself; you are not super-human. A person whose loved one is incarcerated often feels responsible for relieving their misery or even for getting that person out of prison. While each of us has responsibility toward one another, this does not include control of the way a person acts, thinks, or feels. Your loved one is finally and solely responsible for being where he is.

It is true that your loved one can use a lot of help – during incarceration, when seeking parole, and after release. But this does not mean you can or should do everything. Remember that you do not have a magic wand with the power to "fix" everything. It is easy to pressure yourself into taking on more than you can handle or to do more for your loved one than is really good. In the end this will only deplete your limited resources and weaken the prisoner even more.

Keep this in perspective. If your loved one can do something alone, encourage and insist that they do it. It is particularly important for a prisoner to accept responsibility for their own growth and emotional stability. Don't let your loved one or anyone else put you on a guilt trip for failing to do what you cannot do, or for not doing things your loved one must eventually do for himself.

Likewise, you don't have the power to make the police, court, prison, or parole board take any particular kind of action. You might work hard to influence them, but they will ultimately decide what to do about your input. Expecting the criminal justice process to operate in a rational way or expecting too much of yourself and others will only increase your frustration. Therefore, do not feel guilty or responsible for the actions of these agencies. It will only keep you in grief and depression and decrease your usefulness to yourself and your loved one.

Keep a Good Attitude

It is also important to remember that what you are experiencing is a natural reaction. Everyone experiences loss and depression at times in life, although the direct cause may be different than yours. It helps to know that what you are experiencing is natural.

There are other things that can also help. For example, never let depression lead you into feeling sorry for yourself. Never become a "poor me" person; this will just make you your own worst enemy. Realize that depression will pass if you work on it and if you let it pass.

Never become so friendly with depression that you decide you cannot live without it. Don't laugh; people do become dependent on depression and resist giving it up as if it were an old friend. Instead of befriending it, tell yourself the truth. You will live through this experience. You can feel again that you are a good, useful, and worthwhile person with a lot to offer others. You do not need depression as a friend. You can't afford it.

Get Help!

If you have trouble with any of the things noted above, **do not hesitate to get help**. You can get support from friends, ministers, support groups, or other people who care. There are many sources of help available in most communities.

Sometimes your problems may be serious enough that you need help from a trained professional. You may need temporary medication to help you establish good

sleep patterns or overcome intense depression. You may need a professional counselor to help you work through your grief or establish good coping patterns for your
depression.

Aside from negative or crisis reasons, there is much to be said for seeking help for
positive or constructive reasons. If the departure of your loved one demands major
changes – whether economic, social, or personal – in the way you live, it is wise to
seek help in finding job training, new types of employment, and new insights into
yourself and your relationships.

Make sure you get help if you need it! There are many professionals available. If
money is a problem, there are social service agencies that offer competent professional help for a low fee. Getting help from professionals can be part of taking good,
genuine care of yourself. Never hesitate to seek the help you need. You deserve to
have a calm, peaceful, and happy life.

Find a Support Group

Another important resource that can help you deal with grief and depression is a support group. For many of you, the church can fill this need. If faith and religion are important to you, or have been important to you in the past, it may be wise to maintain
or re-establish your involvement with the church of your choice. This can be difficult
if you feel you don't deserve to be a part of the church or that you have somehow let
God down. Again, this is not an unnatural feeling, given the circumstances.

The church, however, has the potential to understand your plight and be a source
of support if you give it a chance. You may hesitate to do this. You may feel the
members will look down on you as a failure, as one who has fallen short of the goals
of the faith group. Again, this could be true of some members of some groups. Most,
however, will want to help.

Do not let your guilt, fear, depression, or anger keep you from reaching out for the
help and support you need. Remember, most faith groups believe that "all have fallen
short of the Glory of God." Chances are, if you don't "poor me" them to death, at
least some members of the group will be willing and able to help you maintain your
sanity and a healthy, realistic perspective on life. If you do not find support in the first
place you try, try another church or faith group.

Even if faith and religion are not important to you, there are other groups in your
community that can help you take care of yourself. Being part of a support group
gives you the chance to help others who are also struggling with losses. Being with
them in their struggles can help you work your way through your own struggles.

Knowing that you can help others and that your help is needed by others is good
medicine for guilt, depression, and the other feelings associated with grief. If you
have never been involved in any group outside your family or closest friends, it can
be doubly important for you to join a support group. The group can be a great help to
you and may be a good source of help for your loved one down the road. People do
need help from each other; it is a natural and healthy process.

If you find that no such group exists in your area, you may wish to start one. This involves finding others with a similar need and then coming together to discuss issues of common concern. Many positive things, such as information sharing, car pooling, and emotional support, can take place in person and over the telephone. Don't sit in a corner and mope; reach out to others who understand and also need help.

Your Relationship With Reality

Grief and the Perspective of Reality

"Hopelessness is self-defeating. Maintaining a negative perspective locks you into grief, frustration, anger, and, ultimately, a hopeless view of the world."

What has been discussed so far deals mainly with what you experience – what you do and feel. Another element in grief is that of perspective. This refers to the meaning or interpretation you put on all the experiences discussed previously. For example, a person in the midst of grief may interpret everything that happens through the influence of depression or anger. In this case, interpretations will inevitably be negative, pessimistic, or even hopeless. That person will interpret even positive or neutral occurrences as negative.

For instance, suppose a parole board's first review decides against your loved one. You might interpret this experience to mean something like, "They are just prejudiced against us. There is no use in doing anything different for the next review because it won't help." If this is your perspective, you will find "proof" of the board's prejudice, regardless of its decisions. If your perspective is negative, you can easily talk yourself or your loved one into avoiding contact with the board because "it will only be a waste of time." This is a self-defeating attitude. A more useful and productive attitude would be, "Even if my loved one is never paroled, it may help to give the board information to support his parole chances."

It is not easy to deal with "set-offs and turn-downs," to be told "We don't have the right person or the right office to deal with your request." When you experience these obstacles, it is very difficult to keep a positive attitude. And it can be especially hard when one bad experience follows another. To help keep your perspective, remember: the vast majority of people sent to prison are eventually released back into the free world, and many of them are released on parole.

A negative perspective may also affect your attitude about other difficulties in your life – for instance, problems at work or with friends. You may think that all of your problems are caused by having a loved one in prison or that there is no way to solve your problems because the world is against you. But these ideas are not true. Problems occur in everyone's life, and they can be endured and overcome.

While in the midst of grief, it is not unusual to have negative perspectives from time to time. The important thing is not to hold onto this perspective so long that you lock yourself into grief. To keep things in a clear and true perspective, remember that your experiences and reactions are natural. You are only being human, and it is normal for you to feel this way. Your main job is to get through the grief and not get stuck in it.

Social Factors

There is another common experience reported by many people who have loved ones incarcerated. You may feel that other people are deliberately avoiding you or are always staring at you. Some people who know about your loved one's situation may stare at you and avoid you. But most people will not. Your feelings are likely a reaction to any shame you may feel.

You may believe that everyone will automatically condemn offenders and all their friends and relations. It is true that some people will judge you to be guilty by association, or guilty for failing to be a "good" parent, spouse, or whatever. Some of these people may even be family members or persons you thought were your friends. But most friends and relatives will not automatically make these types of judgments. If they do judge you, there is probably nothing you can do or say to change their minds. It may be necessary and best if you simply stay away from them as much as possible.

If you feel a distance or coolness from friends or family members, it may not be because they are "judging" you or your incarcerated loved one. Often they may feel uncomfortable with you or your situation. In short, they just don't know what to say or do. And since they don't know how to respond to you, they hold back and try not to get involved.

You can often help them get over their reservations by being honest and displaying a "good attitude." Although there is no guarantee that you can change their response, keeping your sense of humor can be a great help. Humor can be found under almost any circumstances, no matter how grim. Showing that you still have a sense of humor in an awkward or grim situation can put others at ease. This frees them to be natural and supportive of you.

There are people who believe that showing humor under these circumstances is wrong, even sacrilegious. However, if humor can bring you to a clearer, more realistic perspective, and can free others to be supportive of you, I feel it cannot be bad or sacrilegious. So I urge you to find your humorous self, even in the midst of these very trying and unpleasant experiences.

People may also distance themselves from you if you wear your depression on your sleeve. This is especially true if you play "poor me" whenever they are around. Let's face it, "poor me" people are a real drag to be around. But, once you show them you are the same person they have known and that you have a sense of humor, they will likely become friendly and supportive.

Act natural and let your friends and relations know about your trouble, but don't press them about it. Once they are comfortable with you, some of them will prove to be a great help in working through your grief and depression. The people around you can help you keep a hopeful, realistic perspective on your life. And they are often eager to help.

Your Relationship With Your Loved One

Dealing with someone in prison is often difficult at best. For most people, the only regular means of communication is through letters and occasional visits. While these are not the preferred or most effective ways to stay involved with a loved one, they may be the only way. Therefore, you will use them. You will use them because it is important for your relationship that you keep track of what is going on with your loved one and share necessary information. Maintaining regular communication is extremely important to a person in prison, and to you as well. So write regularly even if your loved one does not.

Visits

A visiting room is frequently a crazy, loud, unnatural place to see or visit anyone, let alone those closest to you. There is little privacy, though some prison units have more than others. Without question, jails offer the least privacy. They often give a first-time visitor a real shock. Your first reaction may be, "You've got to be kidding if you think I'm going to visit anyone here!" But this is the facility you must use, so try to get used to it. Plan each visit carefully, especially when there is business to transact. Time is usually limited, so use it well and wisely.

Never assume the visit will be good – or bad. In reality you cannot predict what mood your loved one will be in. You might find them angry and hostile toward you, the jailers, the guards, the warden, other inmates, or the world in general. Or they may be depressed. They may play a good game of "poor me" with you.

Whatever happens during a visit, remember, a prisoner lives in a very unnatural world. A jail or prison is a gigantic container of hostility. Both staff and inmates tend to be hostile. Even though your loved one really looks forward to your visit, you still may get a great deal of hostility or depression dumped on you. Your loved one may be angry or depressed because of something that has happened in the prison. He or she may be angry or play "poor me" because you have not done something you were asked to do, even if the request could not or should not be done.

Often the emotions expressed by your loved one are not really directed at you personally. In fact, it rarely is your fault. Do everything you can to avoid taking the anger or depression personally. And refuse to respond in like manner. Visits are very short and you will soon be able to drive away, so be as understanding as you can.

Be Honest

Another cardinal rule about communicating with your loved one is to be honest and straight about your feelings and about everything you discuss. Above all, never hide anything from your loved one to "protect" him or her. It is most important for your loved one's future adjustment in society to face reality now. Never allow a false picture about what is really going on at home, about plans for release, or anything else. Your loved one may not need to know everything that is going on, but he or she does need to know what is fundamentally important.

Get Good Information

Be prepared for your loved one to tell you stories or pass on advice from other inmates. Such stories and advice may be totally false, or partially or totally true. Your loved one has no way to find out what is true or not true. You will dismiss a lot of this type information because it is clearly untrue. But some of the information will need to be checked for accuracy through other sources. You will have to do this for your loved one. But be discriminating; don't get hooked on trivial or irrelevant issues.

This advice also applies to the things your loved one may ask you to do. Often, their requests are impossible to do, or useless or unnecessary. Inmates can rarely learn the truth about stories or advice by themselves. You are the one who can find out what is useful and not useful, what is possible and not possible, what is necessary and not necessary, what is true and not true. Remember, an inmate does not live in the real world! **You are the chief source of contact with the real world and with truth.** Therefore, you need to have as much accurate information as possible about prison rules, parole regulations, appeals procedures, etc. All inmates suffer from false information and expectations; **you** must be prepared to help your loved one experience reality.

You can't usually prepare in advance for the issues and requests your loved one brings up. But you can get the information after your visit and report your findings in letters. This is one reason it is so important to write regularly and often. Remember, you are your loved one's link with hope, reality, and truth. A big part of your job is to report the facts. Never underestimate the importance of this, even if your loved one has a negative reaction to your information.

Be Prepared

Be aware that a "bad" visit with your loved one or a "bad" letter may throw you back into the grief process after you thought it was over. This is not unusual. If you are rested, healthy, and prepared for ups and downs, you can keep the damage to a minimum. If you are working through the grief cycle, the feelings won't be as intense and they won't last as long as they did at first.

Your reaction to a bad visit or a complaining letter is a good way to tell how well you are dealing with your grief. If you fall back into depression, or if your attitude gets negative, apathetic, or overly angry, it is a sign you are not overcoming your grief. This is especially true if the bad feelings are as intense and last as long as before. In this case, you could probably benefit from some help. So, **go find it!**

Jailhouse Romances

"A treasure chest of love...or a life raft full of holes?"

Some of the personal or romantic relationships between inmates and free world people start or expand after the offender is sent to prison. In fact, new and very powerful ties may develop even when the individuals never knew each other in the free world. Such relationships are unique; they are "not of this world," but they seem to have a special magic all their own. It is like a person from Earth developing a close intimate relationship with a being from Mars.

Developing a long-distance relationship under such conditions can be very romantic, dramatic, and exciting. Each partner offers the best of themselves and hides the worst; each offers or promises what the other one wants (even if it doesn't exist). But these relationships usually lack the elements needed to be successful after incarceration. The partners thrive on fantasy and illusion. They make elaborate plans for the future, but their plans are built on sand and thus highly vulnerable to the tides of reality which follow release from prison.

To be brutally blunt, jailhouse romances make good melodrama but not good sense. Why? Because the factors needed to build a healthy, rewarding intimate relationship are unfortunately absent. This does not mean that two people should not care about each other. They can communicate deeply and share time and energy together. But they should not exceed the bounds of reality. If they do, they set themselves up for great disappointment, grief, anger, and depression when they meet and deal with life after release.

The secret to building a successful relationship during and after incarceration is and always will be **true friendship**. Absolutely nothing else is both possible and appropriate under these circumstances. In fact, such a relationship can be fine, beautiful, and rewarding. But the nitty-gritty of creating an intimate relationship – especially a healthy, lasting male/female relationship – cannot be accomplished until after release. If it is developed well and honestly then, it can become lasting and good.

Too often, however, prison romances remain melodramatic, clinging, dependent, and based on fantasy. This is deadly for the development of a lasting, intimate relationship – one that can deal with the issues of everyday life. A relationship built on illusion does not offer a useful foundation for life together "in the cold light of day." As a result, very few relationships survive the shift from prison to free society.

Therefore, a romantic relationship should be approached with great caution by both the inmate and the person outside of prison. In most cases, such a relationship is best avoided. Predictably, people involved in such interactions will not want to hear this. In fact, they may react with great resentment, telling you that their situation is "special" and lasting. In an effort to prove this, many insist on being married during imprisonment or immediately following release, only to discover they are now legally bound to a total stranger.

If you observe your loved one becoming involved this way, there may be little you can do. However, encourage them to keep a realistic perspective and refer them to reading materials and people who understand this aspect of the incarceration experience.

A Word on Helping Children

Thus far, I have spoken mainly to adults who are members of a prisoner's closest circle of loved ones. Many in this circle, however, are children. These may be sons and daughters, sisters and brothers, nieces and nephews, or grandchildren.

As with an adult, the experience of having a loved one in prison affects a child's life in very important ways. Although the adult who cares for the child may realize this, it is hard to know what the effects will be or how to handle them. The caretaker is often uncertain because he or she doesn't know what the child feels about the situation and isn't sure what the child can understand or do to cope. Besides, the adult is also having difficulty dealing with the situation.

Although nothing has a 100% guarantee of success, the following information and guidelines can help a child cope better with this experience. First of all, remember that children are simply people; they will be affected in much the same ways as adults.

Childhood Development

"As a tree is bent, so does it grow."

Children, even very young children, have the ability to give and receive information and to process that information in order to make sense of the world around them. Some of this information comes from the words and voice tones of the people close to them. Some information comes from what they personally see, hear, smell, taste, and feel. Children, in turn, react and interact with all of this information, which then becomes part of their total experience of life. They use this information to decide how they fit into the world and how they should react to events and the people around them.

From life experiences with others and from their thoughts while alone, children develop answers to some of life's most important questions, such as: *"How do I compare with others?" "What can I expect from others?" "What do others seem to expect from me?" "What do I have to do to keep the tension on me as low as possible in the situation in which I have to live?"*

Of course, the way an infant or very young child processes this information is rather limited and crude compared to the methods a mature, healthy adult might use. Nevertheless, this early processing may strongly influence the final answers a child gives to these questions.

These answers may be based on truth and the way life is generally experienced by most people. If so, a child will tend to have positive experiences and will view life as worthwhile and fun. However, if the answers are untrue or unrealistic for most situations, the child will experience life as confusing, difficult, painful, or depressing.

Different Views of Life

Based on interpretations of early experiences with the people close to them, children may decide that people are not to be trusted because they bring pain, discomfort, and frustration to their life. If children view most people this way in most situations, they may become unsociable, withdrawn, uncooperative, hard to know and get along with, and generally hostile toward society.

On the other hand, a child may decide from early experiences that people are usually friendly and helpful and can be trusted to bring pleasure and relieve pain. This child is likely to make friends and be sociable, cooperative, and outgoing. He or she will want to get close to others and allow others to get close. This child will probably not be hostile toward society.

When a child decides not to trust people, we might think that the child has misinterpreted experiences. However, the child may have had experiences that justify such a negative interpretation. For example, if the people close to the child misunderstood the child's crying, they may have tried feeding when the child was in pain from having colic. In this case, it would be true that the adults did not relieve the child's pain. Or, if the adults are not present when the child needs care, the child may assume that he will always be abandoned by the people close to him.

In these examples, the child's decision was correct at the time. A child can feel the results of the situation, but may not be able to understand the causes. She cannot understand that the adults made a mistake or perhaps could not be present due to sickness, work, or incarceration. Also, a child does not have a wide range of experiences to show that such negative events do not happen all the time. Thus, the child's negative interpretation may become "fixed."

Although the child may have felt hurt or frustrated sometimes or often, it is not true that everyone will hurt or reject the child all the time. But if the child has "fixed" negative answers, he or she will respond negatively to most situations, even if the negative response is not appropriate. These inappropriate responses will continue even after the child is grown. Since he or she gives a negative response for no apparent reason, the child will probably feel "unacceptable" to others. In any situation, no matter how other people respond at first, this person will almost always do something which practically "forces" others to reject him or her.

Thus, a child who develops fixed negative responses to the world will find life unpleasant and unrewarding. It is possible for a person to change his answers to life's questions, but this is hard once these answers are fixed. A child has a much better chance for an enjoyable and satisfying life if the adults caring for them can help the child develop a realistic and positive view of life.

Dealing With Incarceration

*"If **you** can make a positive adjustment to the absence of someone dear, it is more likely that the children in your care will also adjust successfully."*

Just like an adult, a child will be affected by loss when a parent or other loved one is incarcerated. This loss can have a major impact on his/her process of making decisions about life. But the child will also be affected by how the significant adults in their life respond to this loss. The adult's ability to make sense out of what is happening has a strong impact on how a child might deal with their own experience. In fact, the adult can give the child a model from which to learn how to help themselves.

For example, as you, the adult, work through your own depression, anger, frustration, etc., you are showing the child that it is possible to deal with the grief of this experience. If you keep the lines of communication with the child open while you work through your feelings, the child has the chance to see that these feelings can be managed. This will help the child learn some effective ways to deal with painful feelings and cope with life's problems.

By observing your success in overcoming grief and making sense of a confusing and troubling situation, the child can develop a sense of hope. Then, when life feels like the "pits" – hard, painful, and confusing – he can still believe that the unpleasant experiences will eventually pass and be replaced by pleasant experiences once again. With this balanced perspective, the child is more likely to answer the basic questions about life and their place in the world in a positive way.

Guidelines

Guidelines to help a child deal with this experience are simple to state, but may not be easy to carry out.

- **First** – Do not shield the child from the truth about the situation. The child can't make good decisions based on false, inaccurate, or partly true information. You do not need to be brutally frank with the truth. It is usually best to present it slowly, gently, and with compassion.

  It helps if the family and friends who are regularly involved with the child – as well as the incarcerated person – approve of telling the child the truth. However, if you can't get their approval, you need to let them know that you are going to be truthful anyway. In this case, be ready for them to oppose you. But remember, it generally will harm the child in the long run if they are shielded now and have to learn the truth later.

- **Second** – When telling the child the truth, use words, expressions, and actions that the child can understand. This may take a lot of trial and error, but it can be done. Watch the child in other activities, especially in interactions with others.

This will tell you what a particular child can understand. Then you can decide on the best approach to help that child make sense of this difficult situation.

- **Third** – Observe the child the same way you observe yourself. Note any major changes in the child's way of doing things, in their moods, attitudes, etc. This is one of the best ways to detect when someone is having trouble going through the grief cycle. When you see the child is having trouble, try the same things that have helped you to move through your grief.

If your methods don't seem to work for the child, get some advice. Talk to others who have gone through similar experiences with a child, or talk with your parents, grandparents, or friends. If none of this seems to help, go to a professional counselor, physician, or minister.

- **Fourth** – Try to prepare the child for other people's reactions. Friends and acquaintances will certainly find out that the loved one is in prison, and some of them may react negatively. Help the child learn to describe the situation in a way that is honest but still comfortable for the child. At the same time, explain that they do not have to volunteer this information to everyone. You can help the child decide when and to whom the situation should be explained, and when it is not necessary or appropriate to offer this information.

You will need to give the child special support in dealing with other children. He or she must realize that children can be very cruel, particularly when they are in a group. You can help the child find a way to respond to cruel teasing without creating more resentment. In spite of their group behavior, some of these children may become good friends when dealt with alone. It is very important to remind the child that he or she is valuable as an individual: having a loved one in prison does not make the child a bad person.

- **Fifth** – Help the child keep a balanced perspective if the prisoner displays any negative or unpleasant behavior in letters or during visits. Help the child realize the loved one is living in an "unreal" and troubling world. Do not, however, excuse bad or inappropriate behavior by the loved one. Instead, try to help the child differentiate between behavior and the person; explain that they can love the person without liking the behavior. And remember, children tend to copy the behavior they see in parents and other adults who are important to them. Therefore, negative behavior from the prisoner may encourage negative behavior in the child.

- **Sixth** – Do not be startled if a child tries to "manipulate" the situation you are in for their own or the incarcerated one's benefit. Should this occur, talk straight to the child and try to reason things out. If this does not stop the pattern, get help from others, including, if necessary, a professionally trained therapist or physician.

- **Seventh** – Give the child hope. Assure him or her that life will go on and that, no matter what has happened or will happen, life can still be good.

- **Eighth** – Prepare the child for the loved one's return from prison. If the reunion triggers a return of the grieving process, help the child understand what is happening. The child needs to realize that the adjustment may be difficult, not only for the loved one who returns, but for those who have been waiting as well.

In some cases, the prisoner's release may mean that custody of the child will shift from you as caretaker to the returning loved one. This can be a very difficult transition for all of you and should be carefully prepared for in advance. In addition to practical details such as finances, housing, and schools, the change will require a great deal of emotional adjustment for the child, as well as for you and the returning loved one. Often it is better for the releasee to get at least somewhat settled in society and able to deal with his or her own personal adjustments before taking on the added responsibility of caring for a child.

Sometimes a caretaker is unwilling to give up custody because of a strong attachment to the child or because the parent seems unable to care for the child. This decision is a legal as well as a personal issue. It has very serious, long-term results since it affects the relationship between parent and child. It can have a powerful impact on how the parent and child view themselves and their place in the world. If maintaining custody has occurred to you, you should give it extremely careful thought. Then seek the objective advice of competent therapists and legal professionals before taking any further action.

Help is Available

A note of caution. As is true for an adult, a child may seem to work through grief very well and then have a relapse. This is not unusual. Stay calm and retain hope. Keep doing the things that you know have worked for you and the child in the past. Remember, what worked once will probably work again.

Whatever you do to deal with children in this trying situation, remember to consider the level of their capabilities. Do not overestimate what they can do, but do not underestimate it either. Young children can and do solve rather complex problems. It has been my experience that most adults underestimate children's ability rather than overestimate it.

However, it can have a bad effect on a child's development to go to the extreme in either overestimating or underestimating the child's capacity. If you are not sure of yourself in this matter, get advice from people who have more experience with children. It can be very helpful to get assistance from people who are professionally trained in grief resolution and personality development. It is also smart to talk with the child's teacher and school counselor to alert them to the unique needs resulting from this situation.

Dealing With the System

*"The more you know about how the criminal justice system works,
the more you will be able to get from it, and the
more help you can give your loved one."*

Strive to Learn

Learn all you can about how each part of the system works, how to get things done,
who to call, etc. Never give up! You are the most important person in the world to
your loved one. Believe this, even if your loved one has a negative reaction to your
communications or visits.

Dealing with bureaucracy can be highly frustrating, whether it is with a jail, prison, parole board, or any other part of the criminal justice or welfare system. Remember that people who work in these jobs deal with many thousands of clients; they are
often under pressure to do their job without enough staff or money.

To get information or action from any bureaucracy, you will need persistence and
perseverance. Use any resource you can honestly reach. Don't get run off or turned off
by the first person you contact, nor the second, the third, etc. Be creative when you can.
Use humor when you can. Above all, be persistent, polite, and patient. Stick with it.

Pursue Your Rights

You have a right to accurate information and reasonable services, but be careful.
If the person you contact gives you a hard time, acts rude, or fails to do what is required, don't argue with them. You may feel a lot of anger and frustration toward the
bureaucracy or the staff members you contact, but do not vent it on them. This will
rarely help you or your loved one get what you need. Hostility usually only breeds
more hostility.

On the other hand, you should not have to accept abuse or tolerate bad manners
or rudeness. Stand up for yourself and your rights. When dealing with a bureaucracy
like the criminal justice system, it can be hard to find a balance between avoiding
trouble and standing up for yourself. But the effort to find balance can help you build
your confidence and check on your progress in working through your grief.

Again, the key ingredients for successful dealing with the system are patience and
perseverance. Keep trying and you will often find someone else in the same office or
system who can help you. Ask who can tell you what you need to know or who does
have the authority to grant your reasonable request. Then go up the ladder of their
organization until you find someone who will give you the service or information
you are entitled to.

Always keep a record of who you communicate with, what they say, and when.
Get the name and mailing address of key personnel. If necessary, write them a brief,
courteous letter explaining your need or problem and asking how they can help.

Keep a copy of your letter and send the original by certified mail, requesting a signed receipt to be sure they get it. If you don't get an answer in two weeks, follow up with another letter or a direct phone call. If your efforts are blocked by a subordinate, make it clear that you are requesting direct contact with the person in charge. Ask how and when you can get in touch with that person; if the subordinate is still not helpful, ask to be put in touch with his or her immediate supervisor.

Correctional officials should respond professionally to any **reasonable** questions or requests you make. If you do not get a reply after three attempts or the answer isn't reasonable, write to that person's superior asking for help; be sure to enclose copies of the letters you've already mailed and received. Above all, stick with it!

If you are relying on someone for help, do not build up your hopes unrealistically. What Yogi Berra said about a baseball game is also true about bureaucratic decision-making: *"It ain't over until it's over."* Don't count your chickens before they hatch. Keep your perspective and your balance. The people advising you may be competent and well-meaning, but still their forecasts may fail to work out as planned. Be sure to thank people for helping you even a little and, especially, for being civil and polite. A little sugar can go a long way in maintaining a useful relationship.

Top Priority

Remember, your top priority is to **genuinely take care of yourself**. If you work hard at this, you will be able to handle even the most frustrating experiences with the bureaucracy. You may not be able to force the prison or parole board to do what you want or what you think they ought to do, but you **will** feel better about yourself and what you are doing. Your relationship with your loved one will also tend to improve if you take care of your own health and happiness.

Taking genuine care of yourself will keep the grief process on track and **you** in control of your life. The time this takes will be different for each person, sometimes a lot. You may begin to feel normal and be comfortable with your life and its routine. When you get bad visits, complaining letters, setbacks from the parole board or courts, you can take them in stride. You are on top of your world.

You may think all the pain and trauma you have experienced is gone forever. But be cautious; this may not be true. Remember, your loved one is likely among the vast majority of prison inmates who will be released. While release is almost always eagerly awaited, it can also trigger a return of grief experiences.

The Homecoming

"At first they may seem like a stranger, not someone you think you know really well! In truth, they have changed, and so have you."

Coming home is always a major adjustment for those who have been incarcerated. It also requires major changes for those waiting at home. After all the hardship you've been through, you may believe your loved one's return will "fix" whatever problems exist in your life. But don't be surprised if this return actually creates more problems than it fixes.

Reunions

Before imprisonment, you may have been very dependent on the presence and support of your loved one. However, you have been doing without the presence of this person for many months or even years. You have worked hard to create your own way of doing things. You may not be prepared to change your new routines, even for a person you want in your life. And your returning loved one will not be in tune with your current habits and priorities. They may feel threatened and overwhelmed by so much sudden change. As a result, they may try to push people around, to insist on having things their way. They may expect, and even demand, that things go back to the way they were before incarceration.

If you have read "The Correctional Experience" section of this book (pages 40-101, you will have some insight into the reasons for this kind of "power play." Although you understand, you must not accept any form of domination or abuse. This type of behavior will make it impossible to establish a healthy intimate relationship. If such behavior persists, insist that your loved one seek professional help to get their balance. Do **not** tolerate this type of behavior! Establishing a mutually satisfying relationship will require that all participants show a great deal of patience, understanding, and willingness to compromise.

Other members of the household or family may also have significant problems adjusting to the loved one's return. Children often need a lot of time, patience, and support to adapt to the arrival of someone home from prison. Caretakers, and the returning loved one, should do all they can to prepare children for the sudden reappearance of the former prisoner. The reunion should be as smooth, slow, and comfortable as possible, with the children assured that they are safe and loved.

Problems in adjusting to a loved one's sudden reappearance can vary widely among families. You may experience anything from mild annoyance to complete chaos. You may feel your life was finally running rather smoothly by the time your loved one returned, but now things are rough, to say the least. When this happens, you may experience the same feelings you had when your loved one was first incarcerated. Any change in lifestyle or daily routine can be experienced as a significant loss.

Grief Can Start All Over

A return of the grief experience will certainly be frustrating and upsetting, but remember, you worked through it before. If you did it once, you can do it again. If and when you find your grief returning, keep calm, keep your perspective. Make plans to do the kinds of things you did before to take care of yourself. If you have trouble working through the grief experience or run into obstacles putting your plans into action, you may need to get help. A good source of help would be someone professionally trained in grief and family counseling. Again, the first order of business is to take genuine care of yourself. Getting competent outside help may be necessary to accomplish this very important task.

In most cases, if you have resolved the grief problem once, you will not be sidetracked if it returns. But it may catch you by surprise after your loved one's release because you aren't expecting it. Now that you have what you and your loved one wanted most – his or her return from prison – you know you "should" be happy, not upset. But keep in mind that adding another person to your household, especially after a long absence, is a major change in your life. And any major change in the context of living will always create problems that require adjustments. These adjustments, in part, may be experienced as loss, which then may bring a return of the grief experience. This experience could affect anyone who lives in the household.

Remember, this is natural. It is not abnormal for problems to arise when people reunite after an absence. So don't panic! Don't lose your perspective about what is true and real! Do go back to doing the kinds of things that helped you work through your grief before. Be calm and patient with yourself and with others who are involved in the adjustment. Build your "new relationship" on **true friendship**. And if your best efforts fail, do not hesitate to get outside professional help.

A Final Word

In your struggles through the criminal justice maze, you should follow the last part of the Great Commandment, *"Love your neighbor as yourself."* In fact, this commandment simply describes the truth. You need to have love and respect for yourself in order to have love and respect for another. That is why it is so important that you take genuine care of yourself. This care shows that you love and respect yourself. I am not talking about being self-indulgent. Being self-indulgent is not healthy for either the long or the short term; in the long run, it is harmful. But you **must** do what it takes to stay healthy – physically, mentally, emotionally, and spiritually.

If you do take genuine care of yourself, you will be in the best possible position to follow the other universally good rule of life, the Golden Rule: *"Do unto others as you would have them do unto you."* Putting these principles in practice is the best and only way to be of genuine help to your loved one and yourself.

Please remember that no one was born knowing how to deal with the madness of the criminal justice maze. Your survival and growth demand a wealth of soul searching, honesty, and hard work. Keep your hope alive no matter how overwhelmed or depressed you may be. You can endure, and even profit, from the insanity and hardship of this experience. **Be of strong heart!**

Index

The Authors

Ned Rollo

FOR OVER 48 years, Ned Rollo has been active on both sides of the law. Labeled a "habitual criminal," he takes the issue of success after prison very seriously. Following 5½ years in state and federal prisons for manslaughter, narcotics, and firearms violations, he rebuilt his life from scratch. Since earning a degree from Roosevelt University in 1971, he has become a nationally known educator and counselor helping other ex-offenders survive and prosper beyond the criminal justice experience.

Ned founded OPEN, INC. in 1979 to teach survival skills to offenders and their families. To share his hard-won insight, he developed the OPEN Information Series – self-help materials that offer a sometimes painful but always honest view of what is required to rebuild a life in the outside world.

As part of the series, this book is based on the author's direct experience, along with the shared insight of over 50,000 offenders and loved ones he has worked with. Ned has paid the price to learn what it takes to create a meaningful life beyond the shadow of a criminal history. His work, in use across the country, offers a beacon of hope to millions of men and women who are branded as "criminals" and social outcasts.

Louis W. Adams, D. Min.

A minister and licensed professional counselor, Louis W. Adams certainly has the qualifications to help people in crisis. But his unique insight, concern, and sensitivity have made him especially effective as a counselor to offenders and families.

Dr. Adams earned his doctorate of ministry in pastoral counseling from Texas Christian University in 1975. During that time, he gained hands-on experience and practical understanding of the needs of inmates and families while working as a chaplain with the Texas Department of Corrections from 1966 to 1974. He then practiced marriage and family therapy and finally served as director, clinical supervisor, and instructor for the Pastoral Care and Training Center at TCU from 1979 until his retirement in 1991.

Even after he left the prison system, families and people with loved ones in prison continued to seek Dr. Adams' guidance. His compassion and common sense have comforted countless family members and set them on the road to healthy coping.

Ex-Offender Survival and Re-Entry Success Resources

THIS BOOK REPRESENTS A NEW collaborative relationship between Open, Inc. (Offender Preparation & Education Network, Inc.), a nonprofit public service agency, and Impact Publications, a career transition publisher. Founded in 1979 to help motivate and prepare adult offenders to lead productive, responsible, and rewarding lives, Open, Inc. and author Ned Rollo have been responsible for producing several handbooks, audios, and videos designed to assist offenders, family members, and corrections professionals. Impact Publications, founded in 1982 as a career resource center, is a leading publisher and distributor of ex-offender re-entry and correctional materials. Together, these two companies offer the largest collection of books, videos, training materials, instruments, posters, and games designed for ex-offender survival and re-entry success.

The following resources are available from Impact Publications. Full descriptions of each, as well as downloadable catalogs and video clips of many DVDs, can be found at www.impactpublications. com. Complete the following form or list the titles, include shipping (see formula at the end), enclose payment, and send your order to:

IMPACT PUBLICATIONS
9104 Manassas Drive, Suite N
Manassas Park, VA 20111-5211
1-800-361-1055 (orders only)
Tel. 703-361-7300 or Fax 703-335-9486
Email: query@impactpublications.com
Quick & easy online ordering: www.impactpublications.com

Orders from individuals must be prepaid by check, money order, or major credit card. We accept telephone, fax, and email orders. Keep in mind the following rules and practices for shipping materials to correctional institutions. If you're purchasing materials for an inmate, remember, most correctional institutions will not accept packages from individuals. However, as a publisher, Impact Publications is permitted to ship directly to most inmates. In addition, many institutions prohibit inmates from receiving hardback books since such books ostensibly can be weaponized by some inmates (paperbacks are okay). When ordering for a loved one, please double-check on their current location, and include their complete mailing details for USPS and/or UPS delivery (it must include the inmate's assigned number). We normally ship within 48 hours. However, institutions may censor and delay the internal delivery of mail for up to four weeks.

Qty.	TITLES	Price	TOTAL
Featured Products by Ned Rollo			
_____	A Map Through the Maze	$11.95	_____
_____	Ned Rollo's Ex-Offender Survival and Re-Entry Collection (see inside front cover)	369.95	_____
Other Books by Ned Rollo (featured on inside front cover and page 137)			
_____	99 Days and a Get Up	$9.95	_____
_____	99 Days and a Get Up Workbook	14.95	_____
_____	Life Without a Crutch	7.95	_____
_____	Man, I Need a Job	7.95	_____
_____	Necesito Empleo! (Man, I Need a Job in Spanish)	7.95	_____
Training Programs by Ned Rollo (featured on page 137)			
_____	99 Days and a Get Up Training Program	$2,500.00	_____
_____	Life Without a Crutch Training Program	995.95	_____

_____	A Map Through the Maze Program (DVD and Workbooks)	389.95 _____

DVDs by Ned Rollo (featured on inside cover page and page 137)

_____	Preparing for Success: Ex-Offenders in Transition	$79.95 _____
_____	Now What? A Map Through the Maze Orientation DVD	169.95 _____
_____	Why Bother? Finding the Will to Go On	119.95 _____

Re-Entry Pocket Guides (featured on inside back cover page)

_____	The Anger Management Pocket Guide	$2.95 _____
_____	The Quick Job Finding Pocket Guide	2.95 _____
_____	Re-Entry Employment & Life Skills Pocket Guide	2.95 _____
_____	Re-Entry Personal Finance Pocket Guide	2.95 _____
_____	Re-Entry Start-Up Pocket Guide	2.95 _____
_____	Re-Imagining Life on the Outside Pocket Guide	2.95 _____

Re-Entry and Survival for Ex-Offenders

_____	9 to 5 Beats Ten to Life	$20.00 _____
_____	99 Days to Re-Entry Success	4.95 _____
_____	Best Jobs for Ex-Offenders	11.95 _____
_____	Best Resumes and Letters for Ex-Offenders	19.95 _____
_____	Beyond Bars	13.95 _____
_____	Chicken Soup for the Prisoner's Soul	14.95 _____
_____	The Dedicated Ex-Prisoner's Life and Success on the Outside	19.95 _____
_____	Ex-Offender's 30/30 Job Solution	11.95 _____
_____	Ex-Offender's Re-Entry Assistance Directory	29.95 _____
_____	Ex-Offender's Guide to a Responsible Life	15.95 _____
_____	Ex-Offender's Job Interview Guide	11.95 _____
_____	Ex-Offender's Quick Job Hunting Guide	11.95 _____
_____	Ex-Offender's Re-Entry Success Guide	11.95 _____
_____	Houses of Healing	15.00 _____
_____	How to Do Good After Prison	19.95 _____
_____	Jobs for Felons	7.95 _____
_____	Letters to an Incarcerated Brother	16.00 _____
_____	Life Beyond Loss	20.00 _____
_____	No One is Unemployable	29.95 _____
_____	Picking Up the Pieces (for Women)	20.00 _____
_____	Quick Job Search for Ex-Offenders	7.95 _____
_____	Re-Entry Support Programs for Ex-Offenders	40.00 _____
_____	Serving Productive Time	14.95 _____

Personal Finance Guides

_____	The Total Money Makeover	$24.99 _____
_____	The Truth About Money	21.99 _____

Attitude, Motivation, and Inspiration

_____	7 Habits of Highly Effective People	$17.00 _____
_____	30 Lessons for Living	16.00 _____

_____	100 Ways to Motivate Yourself	15.99 _____
_____	The Art of Doing	16.00 _____
_____	Attitude Is Everything	16.99 _____
_____	Awaken the Giant Within	17.99 _____
_____	Breaking the Habit of Being Yourself	16.95 _____
_____	The Bounce Back Book	12.95 _____
_____	Bouncing Back: Rewiring Your Brain	17.95 _____
_____	Can I Get a Do Over?	14.95 _____
_____	Change Your Attitude	16.99 _____
_____	Change Your Thinking, Change Your Life	22.00 _____
_____	Create Your Own Future	21.00 _____
_____	Eat That Frog!	15.95 _____
_____	The Element: How Finding Your Passion Changes Everything	16.00 _____
_____	Finding Your Own North Star	15.00 _____
_____	Free At Last: Daily Meditations By and For Ex-Offenders	15.95 _____
_____	Get Out of Your Own Way: Overcoming Self-Defeating Behavior	15.00 _____
_____	Get the Life You Want	19.95 _____
_____	Goals!	19.95 _____
_____	Healing is a Choice	18.99 _____
_____	How to Save Your Own Life	14.00 _____
_____	How to Win Friends and Influence People	16.95 _____
_____	The Last Lecture	21.95 _____
_____	Magic of Thinking Big	15.99 _____
_____	Making Good Habit, Breaking Bad Habits	19.99 _____
_____	Making Hope Happen	26.00 _____
_____	The Power of Habit	16.00 _____
_____	The Power of Positive Thinking	15.99 _____
_____	Reinventing Your Life	17.00 _____
_____	The Secret	23.95 _____
_____	The Success Principles	18.99 _____
_____	Think and Grow Rich	18.95 _____
_____	What Should I Do With My Life?	16.00 _____
_____	What You're Really Meant to Do	25.00 _____
_____	Wishcraft: How to Get What You Really Want	15.00 _____

Reimagining Your Life With Purpose

_____	Claiming Your Place At the Fire	$16.95 _____
_____	From Age-ing to Sage-ing	15.00 _____
_____	Life Reimagined: Discovering Your New Life Possibilities	16.95 _____
_____	Man's Search for Meaning	9.99 _____
_____	The Power of Purpose	17.95 _____
_____	Repacking Your Bags	17.95 _____
_____	Something to Live For	16.95 _____
_____	Your Best Life Ever	21.99 _____

_____	Your Life Calling: Reimagining the Rest of Your Life	16.00 _____

Mindfulness

_____	The Gifts of Imperfection	$14.95 _____
_____	Mindfulness: A Practical Guide to Awakening	25.95 _____
_____	Mindfulness for Beginners	21.95 _____
_____	Mindfulness for Dummies	26.99 _____
_____	The Mindfulness Solution	16.95 _____
_____	One-Minute Mindfulness	15.95 _____
_____	The Power of Now	15.00 _____
_____	Spiritual Solutions: Answers to Life's Greatest Challenges	22.00 _____
_____	Stillness Speaks	17.00 _____
_____	Super Brain	15.00 _____
_____	Thrive	26.00 _____

Assessment Instruments (packages of 25)

_____	Barriers to Employment Success Inventory	$57.95 _____
_____	Job Survival and Success Scale	53.95 _____
_____	Offender Reintegration Scale	47.95 _____
_____	Transition-to-Work Inventory	54.95 _____

Career Exploration

_____	50 Best Jobs for Your Personality	$17.95 _____
_____	150 Best Jobs for a Secure Future	17.95 _____
_____	150 Best Jobs for Your Skills	17.95 _____
_____	150 Best Low-Stress Jobs	16.95 _____
_____	200 Best Jobs for Introverts	16.95 _____
_____	200 Best Jobs Through Apprenticeships	24.95 _____
_____	250 Best-Paying Jobs	17.95 _____
_____	300 Best Jobs Without a Four-Year Degree	18.95 _____
_____	Best Jobs for the 21st Century	19.95 _____
_____	Occupational Outlook Handbook	19.95 _____
_____	Top 100 Health-Care Careers	25.95 _____

Finding Jobs and Getting Hired

_____	The Ex-Offender's New Job Hunting and Surviving Guide	$19.95 _____
_____	The 2-Hour Job Search	12.99 _____
_____	Guerrilla Marketing for Job Hunters 3.0	21.95 _____
_____	Job Hunting Tips for People With Hot and Not-So-Hot Backgrounds	17.95 _____
_____	Knock 'Em Dead: The Ultimate Job Search Guide	16.99 _____
_____	No One Will Hire Me!	15.95 _____
_____	Overcoming Barriers to Employment	17.95 _____
_____	Unemployed, But Moving On!	13.95 _____
_____	What Color is Your Parachute? (annual edition)	18.99 _____

Career Assessment

	Career Match	$15.00

_____	Discover What You're Best At	15.99 _____
_____	Do What You Are	18.99 _____
_____	Everything Career Tests Book	15.99 _____
_____	Gifts Differing	18.95 _____
_____	Go Put Your Strengths to Work	16.00 _____
_____	I Don't Know What I Want, But I Know It's Not This	15.00 _____
_____	I Want to Do Something Else, But I 'm Not Sure What It Is	15.95 _____
_____	Pathfinder	17.95 _____
_____	What Color Is Your Parachute Workbook	12.99 _____
_____	What Type Am I?	17.00 _____

Resumes and Cover Letters

_____	100 Best Resumes	$20.00 _____
_____	201 Dynamite Job Search Letters	19.95 _____
_____	Best KeyWords for Resumes, Cover Letters, and Interviews	17.95 _____
_____	Best Resumes for People Without a Four-Year Degree	19.95 _____
_____	Blue-Collar Resume and Job Hunting Guide	15.95 _____
_____	Damn Good Resume Guide	11.99 _____
_____	Gallery of Best Resumes for People Without a Four-Year Degree	18.95 _____
_____	Haldane's Best Cover Letters for Professionals	15.95 _____
_____	High Impact Resumes and Letters	19.95 _____
_____	Knock 'Em Dead Cover Letters	14.99 _____
_____	Knock 'Em Dead Resumes	14.99 _____
_____	Nail the Cover Letter	17.95 _____
_____	Nail the Resume!	17.95 _____
_____	The Resume Catalog	19.99 _____
_____	Resumes for Dummies	18.99 _____

Networking and Social Media

_____	Branding Yourself	$24.99 _____
_____	How to Find a Job on LinkedIn, Facebook, Twitter, and Google+	20.00 _____
_____	Job Searching With Social Media for Dummies	19.99 _____
_____	Know 'Em Dead Social Networking	15.99 _____
_____	Networking for People Who Hate Networking	16.95 _____
_____	The Power Formula for LinkedIn Success	16.95 _____
_____	Savvy Networker	16.95 _____
_____	Social Networking for Career Success	20.00 _____

Interviewing

_____	101 Dynamite Questions to Ask At Your Job Interview	$13.95 _____
_____	101 Great Answers to the Toughest Interview Questions	12.99 _____
_____	Best Answers to 202 Job Interview Questions	17.95 _____
_____	I Can't Believe They Asked Me That!	17.95 _____
_____	Job Interview Tips for People With Not-So-Hot Backgrounds	14.95 _____
_____	KeyWords to Nail Your Job Interview	17.95 _____

_____	Knock 'Em Dead Job Interviews	14.95	_____
_____	Nail the Job Interview	17.95	_____
_____	Job Interview for Dummies	17.99	_____
_____	Savvy Interviewing	10.95	_____
_____	Sweaty Palms	13.95	_____
_____	Win the Interview, Win the Job	15.95	_____
_____	You Should Hire Me!	15.95	_____

Salary Negotiations

_____	Get a Raise in 7 Days	$16.95	_____
_____	Give Me More Money!	17.95	_____
_____	Salary Negotiation Tips for Professionals	16.95	_____

Job Keeping and Revitalization

_____	How to Be a Star At Work	$15.00	_____
_____	Love 'Em or Lose 'Em	24.95	_____
_____	Who Gets Promoted, Who Doesn't, and Why	14.95	_____

Start and Manage a Business

_____	The $100,000 Entrepreneur	$19.95	_____
_____	Small Business Start-Up Kit	29.99	_____
_____	Start Your Own Business	24.95	_____

Addiction

_____	12 Hidden Rewards of Making Amends	$14.95	_____
_____	12 Smart Things to Do When the Booze and Drugs Are Gone	14.95	_____
_____	12 Stupid Things That Mess Up Recovery	14.95	_____
_____	Chicken Soup for the Recovering Soul	14.95	_____
_____	Clean: Overcoming Addiction and Ending America's Greatest Tragedy	25.00	_____
_____	Denial Is Not a River in Egypt	13.95	_____
_____	Ending Addiction for Good	14.95	_____
_____	How to Get and Stay Sober	14.95	_____
_____	The Life Recovery Bible	19.99	_____
_____	Life Without a Crutch	7.95	_____
_____	Now What? An Insider's Guide to Addiction and Recovery	14.95	_____
_____	Painkillers, Heroin, and the Road to Sanity	14.95	_____
_____	Passages Through Recovery	14.95	_____
_____	Recover to Live	25.95	_____
_____	The Recovery Book	15.95	_____
_____	Rein in Your Brain	14.95	_____
_____	Stop the Chaos	14.95	_____
_____	The Truth About Addiction and Recovery	16.00	_____
_____	Understanding the Twelve Steps	15.00	_____
_____	You Need Help!	14.95	_____

Anger Management

_____	Anger Control Workbook	$21.95	_____

_____	Anger Management for Dummies	22.99 _____
_____	Anger Management Sourcebook	18.95 _____
_____	Angry Men	14.95
_____	Angry Women	14.95 _____
_____	Beyond Anger: A Guide for Men	15.99 _____
_____	Cage Your Rage for Women	20.00 _____
_____	Cage Your Rage Workbook	25.00 _____
_____	Forgiveness	17.95 _____
_____	Healthy Anger	24.95
_____	Letting Go of Anger	16.95 _____
_____	Managing Teen Anger and Violence	19.95
_____	Pathways to Peace Anger Management Workbook	29.95 _____
_____	Teen Anger Workbook	49.95 _____
_____	Violent No More	24.95 _____

Special Value Kits

_____	71 Re-Entry Success Books for Ex-Offenders	$1,161.95 _____
_____	Anger, Rage, and Recovery Kit	848.00 _____
_____	Discover What You're Best At Kit	428.95 _____
_____	Ex-Offender's Re-Entry Success Library	330.95 _____
_____	Helping Ex-Offenders Achieve Re-Entry Success	373.95 _____
_____	Job Finding With Social Media and Technology Kit	279.95 _____
_____	Learning From Successes and Failures Kit	1,069.95 _____
_____	Mindfulness for Refocusing Your Life Kit	297.95 _____
_____	New Attitudes, Goals, and Motivations Kit	411.95 _____
_____	Overcoming Self-Defeating Behaviors and Bouncing Back Kit	244.95 _____
_____	Reimagining Life: Discovering Your Meaning and Purpose in Life Kit	203.95 _____
_____	Start Your Own Business Kit	316.95 _____
_____	Substance Abuse, Addictive Behaviors, and Recovery Kit	899.95 _____
_____	Tony Robbins "Transform Your Life" Collection	189.95 _____

Survival and Re-Entry Curriculum Programs

_____	99 Days and a Get Up Training Program	$2,500.00 _____
_____	From the Inside Out Curriculum	$599.00 _____
_____	Co-occurring Disorders Program (CDP)	829.00 _____
_____	Life Skills Series for Parolees and Inmates	1,239.00 _____
_____	Life Without a Crutch Training Program	995.00 _____
_____	Map Through the Maze Program	389.95 _____
_____	A New Direction for Ex-Offenders: A Curriculum	4,695.00 _____
_____	Ultimate Re-Entry Success Curriculum Starter Kit	1,795.00 _____

Re-Entry and Survival DVDs

_____	9 to 5 Beats Ten to Life	$95.00 _____
_____	After Prison	149.00 _____
_____	Breaking and Entering...Into a Better Life	199.95 _____

_____	Countdown to Freedom (for men or women)	695.00 _____
_____	Down But Not Out	149.00 _____
_____	Ex-Offenders CAN Ace the Job Interview	179.00 _____
_____	Ex-Offender's Guide to Job Fair Success	129.00 _____
_____	From Prison to Home	`169.95 _____
_____	From Parole to Payroll (3 DVDs)	299.85 _____
_____	From Prison to Paycheck (8 DVDs)	999.00 _____
_____	Life After Prison	99.95 _____
_____	Living Free	149.00 _____
_____	Parole: Getting Out and Staying Out	69.95 _____
_____	Putting the Bars Behind You	99.00 _____
_____	Starting Fresh With a Troubled Background Series	299.95 _____
_____	Stop Recidivism, Now! (3 DVDs)	275.00 _____
_____	Why Bother? Finding the Will to Go On	119.95 _____

Life Skills/Personal Finance DVD/CD Programs

_____	Buying the Basics	$199.00 _____
_____	Effectively Managing Your Money and Work Program	1,170.00 _____
_____	Life Skills for Independent Living CD Program	1,319.00 _____
_____	Life Steps DVD Series	799.95 _____
_____	Managing Your Personal Finances	540.00 _____
_____	On Your Own: Independent Living Skills	99.95 _____

Addiction, Recovery, and Relapse Programs

_____	Addiction Recovery for Ex-Offenders DVD Series	$999.00 _____
_____	Co-Occurring Disorders Program	1,395.00 _____
_____	Substance Abuse and Addictive Behaviors Kit	557.95 _____

                                                      SUBTOTAL _____

TERMS: Individuals must prepay; approved accounts are billed net 30 days. All orders under $100.00 should be prepaid.

Shipping ($5 +8% of SUBTOTAL) _____

                                              TOTAL ORDER _____

RUSH ORDERS: fax, call, or email for more information on any special shipping arrangements and charges.

Bill To:

Name_____Title _____
Address _____
City _____State/Zip _____
Phone (   ) _____ (daytime)
Email _____

Ship To: (if different from "Bill To;" include street address

Name_____Title _____
Address _____
City _____State/Zip _____
Phone (   ) _____ (daytime)
Email _____

Payment Method:

❏ Purchase Order #_____ (attach or fax with this order form)

❏ Check – Make payable to IMPACT PUBLICATIONS

❏ Credit Card: ❏ Visa ❏ MasterCard ❏ AMEX ❏ Discover

Card #												Expiration Date		
Signature							Name on Card (print)							

The Ultimate Re-Entry Success
Curriculum Starter Kit

#7143 Custom-design your own unique re-entry training program with this bestselling set of three DVDs and 225 books. This special kit brings together the best of the best in ex-offender re-entry resources for creating your own powerful re-entry program. Can purchase separately. All new for 2008-2015! **SUPER SPECIAL: $1,795.00 for complete kit of 3 DVDs, 125 workbooks, 75 pocket guides, 25 journals, and 25 directories – a $742.35 savings!**

DVDs *(From Parole to Payroll Series - $299.85)*
- *Finding a Job*
- *Resumes and Job Applications*
- *The Job Interview*

BESTSELLER!

Workbooks (128 pages each)
- *Best Jobs for Ex-Offenders* ($11.95)
- *The Ex-Offender's 30/30 Job Solution* ($11.95)
- *The Ex-Offender's Job Interview Guide* ($11.95)
- *The Ex-Offender's Quick Job Hunting Guide* ($11.95)
- *The Ex-Offender's Re-Entry Success Guide* ($11.95)

Pocket Guides (64 pages each)
- *The Anger Management Pocket Guide* ($2.95)
- *The Re-Entry Employment and Life Skills Pocket Guide* ($2.95)
- *The Re-Entry Personal Finance Pocket Guide* ($2.95)

Planning and Implementation Journal (64 pages)
- *The 99 Days to Re-Entry Success Journal: Your Weekly Planning and Implementation Tool for Staying Out for Good!* ($4.95)

Directory (138 pages)
- *The Ex-Offender's Guide to a Responsible Life* ($15.95)

SCAN ME

Ex-Offender Re-Entry Guides Collection

#6847 Bestselling guides to the whole re-entry process. These five popular workbooks help ex-offenders effectively re-enter society and the workforce. Used by state correctional facilities as key re-entry training resources, each workbook emphasizes taking responsibility, changing attitudes, and making smart decisions. Jam-packed with revealing examples, interactive tests, and insightful exercises. Easy to read and incorporate into ongoing re-entry training programs. 128 pages each. 2009-2016. Can purchase separately at **$11.95 each. SPECIALS: Purchase all 5 re-entry guides *(Ex-Offender Re-Entry Guides)* for $57.95: 10 sets of all 5 guides for $493.00; 25 sets for $1,159.00; 100 sets for $3,697.00.**

- *Best Jobs for Ex-Offenders*
- *The Ex-Offender's 30/30 Job Solution*
- *The Ex-Offender's Job Interview Guide*
- *The Ex-Offender's Quick Job Hunting Guide*
- *The Ex-Offender's Re-Entry Success Guide*

SCAN ME